PERIL.

A Novel.

BY

JESSIE FOTHERGILL,

AUTHOR OF 'THE FIRST VIOLIN,' 'HEALEY,' 'PROBATION,' ETC.

IN THREE VOLUMES.
VOL. III.

LONDON:
RICHARD BENTLEY AND SON,
Publishers in Ordinary to Her Majesty the Queen.
1884.

CONTENTS OF VOL. III.

PERIL.

PART II.—continued.

CHAPTER VIII.

THE TWO LETTERS.

TWO or three weeks had passed since Mrs. Woodfall's arrival at Wiswell Grange, and she had become an established part of the society of the village. Mrs. Trelawney, though she resented and mistrusted her influence over Peril, could hardly allege that as a reason for not visiting her. At her husband's instance she had called upon her, and had come away unable to find any active fault with her, and forced to say that she was 'lady-like and really quite intelligent;' but anyone who knew Mrs.

Trelawney would be aware that into this
seemingly harmless and rather complimentary
phrase she could throw an amount of oppro-
brium and dislike not to be measured by
ordinary standards.   Still, she was as much
of a philosopher as of anything else, and was
'quite intelligent' enough herself to know
that the best way to spoil her own cause and
influence with Peril was to take an openly
inimical tone towards Mrs. Woodfall.   And
she was more anxious than ever to keep that
influence intact, and, if possible, to strengthen
it; for Stephen Harkland had confided to her
that he had never seen anyone to compare
with Miss Nowell, and he was sure he never
should.   He was ready to wait any number
of years for her, but he would never marry
anyone else.

Mrs. Trelawney was delighted; she told
him to leave matters in her hands, and on no
account to speak to Peril at present, as that

would be fatal. He might depend upon her exerting every influence she possessed to aid him ; and one scheme which had already formed itself in her fertile brain was, that when she and her husband went abroad for the autumn and winter, as they hoped to do, Peril should go with them.

'It will be *the* thing for her, and I quite long for the time,' said the astute lady. 'It will remove her from the influence of all these people—this Mrs. Woodfall, whom I thoroughly distrust, Stephen, *for she has got a brother, and he is a widower*—and from her brooding over the wretched past. Let her only get away, and we will see if she does not begin to care for life and for the money that will give her pleasant things in her life. And then, don't you see, if you follow up your present plan you will be travelling too at that time, and——'

'Mrs. Trelawney, you are an angel indeed!'

exclaimed the delighted youth. 'What should I do without you?'

'Well, my dear Stephen, if I must tell you the truth, probably nothing, or less than nothing; you would certainly make a bungle of it, and lose her altogether. Now go and leave me to think all my plans out. You can come to-morrow to tennis.'

But the morrow was wet; a soft, pouring afternoon, such as one has sometimes in July. It was not coldly or maliciously wet : it was a warm, persistent summer rain, which poured gratefully upon the thirsty leaves and grass and flower-beds, and which made the sea look like a great dirty greyish-green smudge on the face of an otherwise verdant earth. Notwithstanding this, Stephen made his appearance at the Rectory, with a somewhat sheepish look. He found the lady of the house seated in her drawing-room with a bright fire in the grate, and a book in her hand. All that he got for his pains was a stringent lecture on his folly for coming on such a day.

'*If* Miss Nowell had been here, as she very easily might,' said Mrs. Trelawney severely, ' it would have been only too palpable, you know ; it would have put me quite out of countenance, and aroused suspicions, and all sorts of things. As it is, there is no harm done, for I don't think she will come. You may have some tea, and then you must go back, and I will not let her know how silly you have been.'

Crestfallen, and with ardour damped, Stephen accepted the cup that was handed to him, and betook himself to his home as soon as might be. He and Mrs. Trelawney were, no doubt, a clever and a charming pair of plotters ; but they miscalculated—he, because he was ignorant of Peril's heart, and her object in life ; she, because, though knowing those things, she had her own object so large before her eyes that it dwarfed all others, and made them appear dispropor- tionately small, and so she failed to give due significance to what should have been im- portant factors in her calculation. Even while she and Stephen sat together in her drawing-room, Peril Nowell was alone in her bedroom at Stanesacre, writing a letter which, after long wrestling within herself, she had brought herself to do. She did not so easily forget her loves and her hates; she was far more tenacious of her purposes, when they had once been formed, than it was convenient for Mrs. Trelawney to admit to herself. She had yielded to that lady in many things, she was sincerely attached to her, really fascinated by her; but her own schemes only slumbered, her own view of things was still the view she took. It was upon this view that she acted, when she felt that the time for action had come. It was inevitable that it should be so; impossible that it could be otherwise.

She sat at a little table by the open window with her writing-materials before her, and before she began to write she listened long to the falling summer rain, and to its steady patter upon the motionless leaves. But when she did begin to write, it was out of the depths of her heart. There was no pausing, no hesitating, no reforming of sentences, or crossing out of words. It was as if she took what she had to say in a solid piece from her heart, and stretched it forth upon the paper with a pen which could hardly fly fast enough to write the words.

'Stanesacre, Wiswell,

'July 10th, 18—.

'My dear Cousin,

'(I suppose you will not deny me that name, though we seem to have been parted now in a way that is terrible to me)—You will know, if you have seen your friend Mr. Lawford lately, that his sister, Mrs. Woodfall, and his little boy, are living for the summer at his house here. I have seen them often, and from them I have heard the only news that I have had of you. I told Mr. Hankinson, when I was miserable and unhappy, at the time I was leaving Darkingford, to tell me nothing except purely business things, and he has obeyed my words to the letter. Mrs. Woodfall tells me that you have taken the course of learning a trade, and that you are going to Australia to ply it there ; and that sometime, when you consider you are entitled to do so, you are going to return and marry Miss Hankinson. I cannot tell you the feelings with which I have heard of this resolution of yours. It fills me with pain and with misery. It is not right—it is not just—it is not fit that this should be so. Miss Hankinson must love you very much, but oh, not wisely, to consent to such an arrangement. Forgive me saying these things; it is because I feel from the bottom of my heart the wretched wrong that makes them possible, that I write as I do. Hugh, I will speak out—it is best—it is right; and I am so miserable when I think of what my silence and standing aloof may cost, that I will cast aside every consideration of fear. You have been wronged, I know you have, and by me. It is a truth which has been present with me, and has been a torment to me, in every one of my waking hours since I knew that wrong had been consummated. What makes it the more agonizing and bitter is, that so far from wishing to wrong you, I loved you with all my heart and soul, as the one person who had shown me kindness and consideration in a life, and in a house, which I abhorred. But have I sinned irreparably? Am I to be punished all my life for one mistake, one fit of passion, one single crime? Why, they hang even a murderer, and put him out of his misery; they let off the man who is doomed to penal servitude for life, after he has behaved himself seemingly for a certain time: and must I carry my punishment with me for ever? Surely you, who used to seem to me so tender-hearted, cannot mean this; you cannot, you cannot! You will say, for you were always logical, and always made me give my reasons for things—when I had any—you will say: " Let me hear what you propose to do." That is what I am going to do. I beg you to be patient, and consider what I say, to the end. If there are business mistakes in my plan they arise from my ignorance, and you will know how to set them right.

' This is what I want you to do. When I am of age, I gather from the will that I become practically the mistress of my grandfather's

money and property. Mr. Hankinson is
only the manager in it. Now, I, if I like, as
I am the head of the firm, can take a partner
in it, and why should not you be that partner ?
what more natural or reasonable ?—you, who
have for so many years been engaged in that
very business. By this means will be done
away with all the appearance of a *gift* which
might arise if I divided the fortune with you,
and which you refused to let me do. I am
so ignorant of business, that I do not know
what obstacles there may be to this. It is
what I should like the best; but if there is
any insuperable difficulty in the way of it, let
us have some other plan : let us call you my
agent, or my secretary, but let you be practically the sharer of the half of this money and
property. You, who know all about business
and such things, will easily see how something
can be arranged. Do not go away ! Do not
banish yourself and punish me thus : I do not

feel as if I could bear it.   Show this letter to
Miss Hankinson; she has a clear head, and
a man's understanding, as I have heard, and
so I could imagine.   But she has a woman's
heart, I am sure, and if it does not agree with
my wish, and say it is not only just but good,
I shall indeed be surprised.   Let her know,
unreservedly, that to make right the wrong
that has been done, is what I wish for now.
Let her know the reason—I am past feeling
shame on that point—she will know how all
pride has been burnt out of me when I say it
is because I did love you as she loves you
now, and because I do love you—I swear
it, just as my Bible bids me—as my neighbour,
as myself.

‘ I know you are proud, I know it may cost
your pride a little pang.   Think how mine
must have been trailed in the dust before I
could write this, and bear in mind that by
this one small sacrifice you will make a very

unhappy woman contented and reconciled with her lot in life. I again say, ask Margaret. I know, I feel convinced that she will agree with me. I await your reply—I need not tell you how—and I am,

'Your faithful Cousin,

'PERIL NOWELL.'

She did not trust herself to read it through— it was as flesh of her flesh, and blood of her blood ; and she felt as if she throbbed and shook from head to foot, body and soul alike, when it had been torn from her. It was the outcome of a fortnight's tortured thought, and musing, and brooding—ay, and prayer during long vigils when no one knew that she wakened.

It must be posted by her hand, and hers alone. She almost dreaded to trust it to the post, along with other letters. Surely it would cry out and bleed, or give some visible sign of the agony with which it had been, as it were, plucked from her. She sealed it, stamped it, and looked at her watch. The post went out very early—before four in the afternoon—from that out-of-the-way spot. She put on her hat, took the precious letter in her hand, and sallied forth into the village to post it.

Down the perpendicular hill, with the extraordinary little red-roofed houses, which seemed built on successive shelves on the sides of it, into the heart of the queer little village. She dropped the letter in the box: the messenger was sent with prayers and tears if ever messenger was. Now that it was gone, she felt a dead, dull apathy succeed to her feverish excitement. She would live in such an apathy, concealing it as best she could from those who surrounded her, until the answer came. Of its import she had little doubt. ‘Grief may endure for a night, but

joy cometh in the morning.'   Hugh would be
stayed by her letter when he showed it to
Margaret Hankinson.   Her cause was as
good as gained.   She remembered Margaret's
eyes; those beautiful, limpid, clear grey eyes,
so candid, so strong, and so true, which looked
as if they could see into one's heart; could
see through all intricacies and complexities,
right into the soul and centre of a thing.
They would see straight enough in this case,
she was sure.   A woman who had spent so
much of her strength and her time as
Margaret Hankinson had spent, in minister-
ing to the poor and wretched, the fallen and
the wicked, would be able to discern the
extent of Peril Nowell's fault, and would tell
her lover what was the true and the right
course for him to take.

She received an answer almost sooner than
she expected, on the day but one following.
It lay on her plate on the breakfast-table, but

she dared not read it then. She slipped out of the house, round by the back of the farm, and on to the cliff, and when she could see neither tree nor chimney, nor any sign of human neighbourhood, she sat her down to read.

'Barton Street, Darkingford,

'July 11th, 18—.

'MY DEAR PERIL,

'Your letter has distressed me more than I could tell you, for I perceive from it how needlessly you are troubling yourself on my account. My fate was decided, and your fate was decided, in my grandfather's will. Were I able to veer round, first this way and then that, shifted about by every wind of fortune, I might as well lay me down and die at once. I took my resolution almost immediately; it has never swerved since. Do not be unhappy—I am not. I feel free, and I am not afraid of life or of the future. I am independent : if I did what you wish me to do, I should be chained and fettered on every side. I wish I could write the words " I decline it," as gently as I would say them if you were here, and could make you understand, by a letter, how grateful I feel for your generosity. Consider that I have spoken gently, my dear cousin, but without any intention of changing. So firm is my resolve that I shall not open up discussion, or pain Margaret by showing her your letter. I wish you a long, a prosperous, and a happy life, and that you may enjoy the fortune which no doubt you are much better suited to possess than I am. And, with every consideration, I would suggest that this should be the last word between us, on this, or other matters.

' I am,

' Your Cousin,

' HUGH NOWELL.'

42—2

Peril had been, as it were, driven to her
feet again as she read these words, and
they seemed to beat like blocks of stone upon
her heart—cold, and hard, and unsympa-
thetic—with unflinching resolution, unyielding
egotism, so it seemed to her, in every syllable
of every line.   To bring this upon herself
she had written that letter with her heart's
blood, with shame and anguish, and out of a
supreme passionate desire that right might
be done.   She had sent it, not only for him,
but that it might meet the eyes of a pure-
hearted and a large-hearted woman, and plead
her cause with her.   That woman was to be
kept in ignorance.   The eyes of this man,
who was so dense and so bigoted, were not to
be opened by the only hand which could open
them: he, and he alone, had read her agonized
confession, and had doubtless wondered what
in the world her sentimental fancies had to do
with the matter at issue.   She had laid bare

her heart, exposed her weakness, her folly, her secret thoughts and longings, to a pair of eyes as cold as they were dull : she felt as if every drop of blood in her veins turned into fire, as she realized it, and burnt her up, and scorched her with a shame and a humiliation which was intolerable. If anyone who had understood had inflicted the chastisement— but that he did not understand was visible, patent, crying aloud in every word that he had written to her.

'You will not,' she said to herself at last, between her set teeth. 'We will see ! We will see if I cannot *make* you—dolt !'

She folded up the letter carefully, and with a very disagreeable smile upon her lips ; put it into her pocket, and turned homewards. From this time all that Peril did was done, not because any spark of love for Nowell remained in her heart, but because she was resolved to be rid of the burthen that she loathed ; because she felt that she had been treated ungenerously and unjustly, and was determined to cast from her all which clung to her as a sign of her own sin.

'Money will do most things,' she said within herself, as she took her way to Stanesacre. 'We will see if it will not even get rid of money. But patience, patience—I will bide my time.'

CHAPTER IX.

THE RETURN.

THE pomp and splendour of mid-September were over all the land. Warm skies of a soft blue, which seemed to have a filmy veil of the finest grey gauze drawn between them and the eyes below that looked up to them—a sea of emerald or sapphire, according to the state of sky or sun, or time of day—a delicious heat, and calm, and mellowness, such as in England one often fails to get in June, and receives in September in double beauty. It was late in the afternoon of a day like this, when Peril Nowell, and Mrs. Woodfall, and

their charge Humphrey began to move about
as if they were thinking that the time had
come for wandering homewards. The place
in which they had ensconced themselves was
as fair as place could be. Leaving Wiswell
Grange, they could go, first down a sort of
gully or lane, very sheltered, and deeply sunk
between high banks, then along a steep,
rough path winding about the face of the
cliff down on to the shore. Proceeding a
little northwards, they rounded the shoulder
of a mighty black cliff, and found themselves
in a delicious little bay, paved with shining
yellow sand, in which were many still, crystal
pools lying in the hollows formed by rough
black stones, covered with seaweed. Under
the sheltering sides of these stones, and in
the clear water, and around the edges of it,
was a perfect paradise of marine treasures—a
very Golconda to little Humphrey, who, with
his spade and his tin pail, asked nothing

better than to spend the entire day in this place. The anemones; the prickly, bristling urchins; the brilliant coral-hued and rosy star-fish of all sizes which lay around; quivering lumps of jelly-fish, too; and waving in the pools, forests of fairy seaweed, of every hue and every shape, but all of a delicacy no human hand could ever hope to imitate, and of colours blended and harmonized by the in-fallible artist Nature—these offered joys to the little town-bred boy which he had never known before, and of which he was never weary. His companions were almost equally enthusiastic, partly out of delight in his delight, partly because here and in these sur-roundings they too felt the beauty of the things, and their importance, and delighted in them, and wished for nothing more; or perhaps, to their more sophisticated minds there came the sad thought that if seaweeds and anemones were not exactly things conveying the highest delight, and that best worth having, yet, that so long as life withheld the heaviness of her hand and gave them nothing worse, they might count themselves happy.

They had brought lunch in a basket, and had been here ever since noon. Peril had also brought a book, and had been part of the time reading to Katty, who, on her part, had been absorbed in a water-colour drawing of a fine black rock called Black Nab, which rose to the north, standing boldly out in the water, with the surges curling crisply about it. It was the home of many sea-birds, and was an object upon which Peril had loved to gaze ever since she came to Wiswell.

'There!' said Mrs. Woodfall, after a long and studious silence, during which she had painted, and Peril, having cast her book aside, had been gazing at the distant tide, and listening to its murmur. 'Give me your candid opinion, Peril.'

She held the sketch up, and Peril looked at it. It was undoubtedly spirited and good.

'I think it is splendid. I wish I could do that : it must take your mind away from itself so much.'

'It has been an unspeakable consolation to me, and I have thanked the Giver for it many a time,' said Katty, her bright eyes looking with a shimmer of contentment in them from her somewhat hollow face ; she was one of the women who, while always comely, become thin and hollow in their struggle with life. She had clear, good features, and fine grey eyes, but the cheeks were sunken, and the figure, which one could see must once have been most graceful and most attractive, had wasted — it was thin; the bloom had gone, but the grace and the graciousness remained with her, and always would.

'You have many more,' said Peril—' some

I like even better than that; why do you not
frame them and hang them up?   Think how
they would brighten up the dark walls of the
old Grange.'

'My dear child, do you mean to say that
you are under the delusion that I can afford
to fritter away my time painting pictures to
hang up in my drawing-room?   When I've
got a thousand a year, I promise you I will
make it look pretty enough.'

'But, if you paint them, why not hang
them up?   It seems to me to come to the
same thing.   It is still more wasteful to paint
them and put them away, than to paint them
and hang them up.'

'What sweet simplicity!   I do not paint
them and put them away.   I paint them, and
send them to London to a man who tries to
sell them for me.'

'Oh, Katty!' exclaimed Peril, a deep flush
crossing her face; 'and you let me take those

two nice ones, and you never said a word. How could you! I will give you them back at once.'

'Bless your heart, you are very welcome to them! I am not so poor that I can't afford a gift now and then; or rather, I should say, I am so poor that when I give a present, I have to fashion it with my own hands. But I'm sure that won't lessen the value in your eyes.'

'It will enhance it tenfold; but I feel as if I had done such a greedy thing, in seizing upon them in that way. Only I did not know.'

'I know that,' said Mrs. Woodfall, dabbing in another touch or two. 'How exquisite the light is just at that corner, do you see?—it brings out a sort of colour on that edge of the rock—like polished bronze with some green in it—heavenly, and it makes one despair; how can one ever do a thing like that?'

' I think you have given it wonderfully.
But, Katty, tell me, this man that you send
your pictures to, does he pay you well for
them ?'

' Not so well as I could wish ; but then he
sometimes has difficulties in selling them at
all.   Perhaps I may get a couple of guineas
for this.'

' Oh, what a shame !   I am certain it is
worth ten pounds, at the very least.'

' A thing is worth what it will fetch,' said
Katty philosophically ; 'at least that is what
all practical people tell me.'

' They tell a very great untruth.   I wonder
what a kind word or a generous deed would
fetch in the market,' said Peril contemptuously.
' Yet it might be worth fortunes.'

' Ah, yes !   Practical people don't count
those little items.   All the same, my dear, I
agree with you.   A kind look could hardly be
made the nucleus of a limited company with

a capital of one hundred thousand pounds in ten thousand shares of ten pounds each, fully paid up; but, especially to poor little diminutive property-holders like poor women, it may mean a great deal more than that.'

' I do not like what you say about painting those beautiful pictures, and selling them for money.'

' Don't you ? I like it very much—when I get the money. It helps me in my house-keeping here, because my poor dear husband just now has got so very little money that he can give me none, practically speaking. I have what I earn in this way, and what Paul gives me for Humphrey; but when Humphrey begins to go to school, you know it will be a bad look-out for both Paul and me, unless poor dear Paul gets on very well in that office of yours at Darkingford.'

' Don't—don't—call it mine,' said Peril, wincing, while a vexed, sore feeling stole over

her heart—the feeling that if Hugh Nowell
had behaved with common generosity he
might have had so much authority in the
affairs of that office as to have materially
advanced Paul Lawford's interests.

'Well, I won't,' said Katty. 'And now it
is time to go home. Where is the youth?
Oh, there! Doesn't he look bonny, Peril, and
the picture of health as he stands in that
pool with his clothes tucked up, and his
beautiful bare legs—Humphrey!'

'Yes!' came wafted upon the breeze in
Humphrey's voice.

'It's time to go home. Come out of that
water, and let your garments down, and put
on your shoes and stockings.'

Reluctance was expressed in every line of
Humphrey's figure, but he splashed out of his
pool, and skimmed over the sands towards
them.

'Now then!' observed his aunt Katty.

'Yes, yes,' said Humphrey, reproaching her impatience. 'I must wait till my legs are dry' (indignantly); 'and you haven't got a towel.'

'Very well; the best way to dry your legs is to run about in the air—so be quick.'

Nothing loth, Master Humphrey flew along the sands, with his perfect young limbs twinkling in the sunshine.

'Primitive,' observed Katty. 'But I do despise milksoppy boys, and so does his father.'

'Does he? I should have thought——'

'I know what you mean. You think Paul the quintessence of lazy indifference, and you think he is a little bit of a—not a milksop, but——'

'Well, he did not seem to me as if he were fond of anything very active.'

'He has that indifferent way. But I would defy you to say you ever saw him looking

stupid or silly, or as if he would be helpless
when he was needed. That's what I mean.
When he is with us, he makes Humphrey do
all sorts of things—rather severe taxes upon
his little patience and fortitude, I think sometimes ; but the boy adores him, simply.'

'Yes,' said Peril vaguely, as Humphrey,
who certainly looked a model of childish
health and strength and beauty too, came up
to them, squatted upon the sand, and remark-
ing that he was now quite dry, proceeded to
put on his shoes and stockings.

'You are a broth of a boy !' said Katty,
making a sudden snatch at his curly head and
rosy face ; 'but I wish the sun did not turn
you so brown, child. You will be as bad as
your dad was when he came home from
India.'

Humphrey stopped abruptly in the midst
of his toilette, and asked :

'When will my dad come here to see us ?'

'Oh, I don't know. Not yet. He is too busy. He's working for you, Humphrey, you know.'

Humphrey gave the subject a few moments' consideration, and then pulled on his second stocking.

'I've got three live crabs,' he remarked. 'I filled my pail with salt water, and I'm going to carry them home, and keep them all night in it.'

'Well, remember they will most likely be dead in the morning ; and if they are, you must not bring any more away—do you understand ?'

'I don't think they'll be dead. They look very strong.'

'But do you understand ?'

'Yes—oh yes.'

'Very well. Are you ready ? What a little sight you are !' kissing him with ardour. 'Come along, if Miss Nowell is ready.'

'Are you ready, Miss Nowell ?'

'Yes, dear.   No,' as he offered to take her book and carry it for her; 'look after your little crabs.'

'Are you coming to have tea with us, Miss Nowell?'

'Yes, if you've no objection.'

'What an idea!' said Humphrey, as if he were shocked.   Then, looking down into the pail in which the crabs were struggling— 'They look very strong, Aunt Katty.   I think they will be alive to-morrow morning.'

'I don't,' said she decidedly; 'I think they will have torn each other to pieces long before then.   But go along; you can but try the experiment.'

'No,' said Humphrey, trotting on in front; 'we can but try the exempriment.'

Stifling their laughter, his aunt and his visitor made no reply to this judicial utterance, but followed him up the rocky path.

Peril gave a furtive side-glance at the

Rectory gates as they passed them on their way to the Grange.

'I hope Mrs. Trelawney won't think I have neglected her.'

'Why should she? You go there nearly every day.'

'She has been so wonderfully good to me. She wants me to go abroad with them in the winter—at least, for the winter.'

'Do you think you will?'

'Perhaps—I don't know. I feel as if I didn't much care what I do.'

'You must not get like that.'

'Well, it is only by fits and starts. I know very well what I have to do. I'm only waiting for the opportunity of carrying it out.'

But she knew that Mrs. Trelawney would not be too well pleased at her having spent an entire day without going to see her, and she arranged in her own mind to leave the

Grange early, and call at the Rectory on her way to Stanesacre.

They turned in at the gate of the drive which led up to Wiswell Grange. It was a damp, dank kind of avenue of trees, which were unusually large and flourishing for that part of the world. This arose from the fact that the house and its entire grounds lay a little below the level of the road, and were perfectly sheltered from the east, and very much from the north. It was also a very, very ancient house, this melancholy, little old Grange. It had been for hundreds of years in possession of this same family, and they had kept this shell and husk, as it were, of their former estate and comfort, while the revenues thereof dwindled and became smaller every year. It was not exactly dilapidated, for it was very solidly and strongly built, and did not easily fall into decay; but it was neglected, not from want of will, but from want of means to keep it up. The garden-walks, and some of the beds too, were overgrown ; such flowers as there were, were hardy, old-fashioned perennials, which had taken hold of the soil and struggled upwards and bloomed year after year, in standing protest against adverse circumstances. There were, just now, some gaily coloured asters ; some spikes of the blood-red gladiolus shooting up, like sudden flames, in a shady corner ; some struggling tufts of a fine large crimson carnation ; and a bush or two of late, hardy roses. For perfume there was mignonette, which threw its incense upon the air, and some bushes of lad's-love, and here and there a snapdragon. There was a charm about this old garden, melancholy though it was ; it was so still, so lonely, and so self-contained. Being situated in a hollow, the only view one had from the windows of the old grey house was the garden, and from the garden—unless one went to the gate of set purpose, and gazed up and down the turnpike-road, one saw nothing but the old house, its little deep-sunk lattices catching the gleam of the setting sun, and shining through the trees like eyes watching, both grave and bright.

Along this melancholy avenue did the two women and the little boy go towards the house. Once inside its thick old walls, the forlornness seemed to vanish. Everything was very old—a great deal of it was very worn and very poor ; but Mrs. Woodfall's magic touch had made the poverty beautiful, instead of sordid. Diving into the old cupboards, she had dragged forth what she called 'pots in abundance'—old things which had been stowed away, as cracked or old, and left to the ravages of dust and cobwebs. To wash them, and sort them, and pick out the best of them, had been the work of a forenoon with Katty, and had produced a result of

abiding grace and cheerfulness. She had
left the sombre old prints and paintings—
prints which Charles Lamb might have mistaken for some of those Hogarth ones which
adorned—so inappropriately, as he said—the
walls of his parlour—paintings of which the
less said the better, belonging probably to the
'great tea-board school.' In the deep old
fireplace during the hot days of summer,
Katty had had a bunch of green ferns and
flowers; but on this September evening,
when the night was sharp, whatever the day
might have been, there burnt a hot peat-fire,
and with it came the peculiar smoky odour
which such a fire always produces. · The table
was spread for the evening meal; the place
looked comfortable, and cosy, and cheery, if it
were worn and shabby, and old into the
bargain. Do I linger too long over the oft-told
tale of a fallen old house, with its neglected
wilderness of a garden, and its few poor trea-

sures of rickety old oak, and cracked old family
crockery ? One has heard of such things
before, truly ; and one has heard of palaces
where the atmosphere is less kindly and the
hospitality less genuine.

Their entrance with laugh, and ringing
voices, and clatter of umbrellas and spades
put down, and bustle of Humphrey with his
tin pail and his three precious crabs, woke a
new life in the still old house. Katty's maidservant emerged from the kitchen regions—a
gawky girl, who had developed in these few
weeks, under Mrs. Woodfall's able manipula-
tion, into a respectable country maid-of-all-
work, and had got an air and—so her friends
said—' a style about her ' which neither they
nor she had ever anticipated for her. She
received sundry orders from her mistress,
and then there was a pilgrimage upstairs, to
repair the ravages made by sand and wind
and general skirmishing in the open air, and

another deep silence while these ceremonies were in operation.

Humphrey was the first to re-appear on the stage of the parlour, where the table was spread, looking a nice little gentleman enough in his dark blue suit, and with his shining hair assiduously smoothed. Anna, the maid, was just carrying in a dish with cold meat on it, which she laid on the table. Humphrey prowled round, with his hands in his pockets, and a soothing luxury of anticipation made itself felt within him.

'I am so hungry, Anna.'

'I dare say, Master Humphrey. You'll be free enough with your victuals to-night.'

'I wish they would come down. I think I shall read till they do. Then, perhaps, I shan't feel so hungry.'

With this laudable determination he took a book, and turned his back upon the table. It was a course which his father had once recommended to him as being a prudent one, when one had to wait.

Peril came next, and found him there, and then Katty, and they seated themselves; Humphrey taking the foot of the table, and doing the host with all imaginable quaintness and grace.

'Let us go into the garden,' observed Katty, when the meal was over, 'while she takes the things away. It is too cold in the drawing-room, and I can't afford two fires at once.'

They went out; it was still daylight, and not seven o'clock. The fires of the west were glowing yet, and the air was still warm after the mellow, balmy day.

Peril was dressed in one of those 'white summer dresses' which Mrs. Trelawney had been desirous for her to have. Her white face, above her white dress, made her dark eyes and dusky hair look deeper still. She plucked one of the deep red roses and stuck it in the bosom of her dress, and paced about with Katty for a little while. Humphrey went to swing on the gate, a favourite pastime of his; and by-and-by Peril went into the house again, and stole towards a very tinkling old piano which stood in the parlour—a very sad and deplorable old instrument, which could have known no tuner's fingers for many a year. Out of it she managed to extract some notes which pleased her, and finding that the room was empty, she opened it, and ran her fingers over the keys, and had been wandering in and out of various sad and intricate little harmonies for some little time, when Katty's voice came in at the open window:

'Sing "Mignon" for me, Peril, and I will walk about here and cry; it is what I should enjoy more than anything.'

This song was peculiarly suited to Peril's

voice and style, and she sang it, on the rare occasions when she did sing, *con amore.* Its mystic sadness appealed to her as no other song that she knew—and others, as well as Mrs. Woodfall, might have found that tears were forced from them by the passion and the pathos with which that voice asked the longing question :

> ‘ Kennst du das Land?
> Kennst du es wohl ?’

And the strength of the yearning with which the last notes swelled out :

> ‘ Dahin, dahin, möcht’ ich mit dir,
> O mein Beschützer, ziehen !’

‘ *Dahin ! wohin ?*’ was the question she asked herself, as the notes died away, and she folded her hands on her lap, and let the crowd of thoughts, which this song always aroused, flow into her mind. ‘ Thither—but where ?’ It was what she had asked herself of herself all her sad young life, and had got no answer yet.

There was a sort of noise and bustle outside; laughing, talking, and — not crying, surely not crying, but a sort of incoherent, wild bustle, and then a voice which thrilled her, and brought memories recent, bitter, yet not because of anything it had ever said. Rather, it had tried to soothe her.

'Well, my dear little lad, don't smother me. Save me alive,' said this voice, laughing and caressing. And then came Katty's; and they all surged nearer to the door, and nearer to her.

'Come in! come in! To think that you have *walked* all the way from Foulhaven!'

And then it seemed they were all in the parlour—all three of them; Paul, with Humphrey half on his shoulder, half in his arms, doing his best to smother him; Katty hang-

ing on his arm, radiant delight in each of the
faces.

Peril felt her heart stabbed—felt herself a
discordance, a disturbance : not wanted on
the scene. She rose, silently, like a tall
white ghost out of the dusk in the corner.
Lawford saw her, and stopped abruptly in
his laughter.

' Peril, did you ever know such a thing !'
exclaimed Mrs. Woodfall, and her voice was
vibrating, had tears in it. 'And we were
talking about him this very afternoon. I was
just beginning to cry over your song, when
he lifted the latch of the gate and walked in.'

'Never expecting to find you here,' said
Paul, releasing his right hand, and going up
to her.

Peril put hers into it silently. It was very
like a dream—and yet how real !

CHAPTER X.

FORECASTING.

'SO you walked all the way,' repeated Katty.

'You seem to think I am much to be pitied on that account. I can tell you it was splendid—after Darkingford. I found, on inquiring at Foulhaven, that "flies," as they call them, cost a small fortune ; and there is a carrier's cart——'

'Yes,' interrupted Humphrey, 'and he goes past here at nine o'clock *every* night with a lantern, when I'm asleep.'

'I'm glad you pass your time in such a becoming manner,' said his father. 'So I engaged the carrier, by a solemn vow, to convey my luggage hither this night, and——'

'He is a dear old thing,' interrupted Katty. 'He conveyed my few valuables up here, soon after I came; and as it was a large undertaking, he sent me in a written bill, "To delivering 1 cart load of gods." I nearly died with laughing while I was paying him.'

Mrs. Woodfall had another good fit of laughter at the recollection, and it struck Peril how very funny it was, that instead of solicitous inquiries after each other's health and welfare, they should immediately on meeting begin to recount the eccentricities of the village carrier.

'Well, my "gods" will take up only a very small corner of his cart,' remarked Paul, with a smile; upon hearing which Katty seemed to remind herself that his coming was quite unexpected, and she said quickly:

'But tell me, Paul, why have you come? Have you a holiday, or——'

'I am sure you will want to hear all Mr. Lawford's news, Katty,' said Peril, rising, with somewhat of an effort; for she would gladly have escaped all notice if she could, but felt that the time was come to speak. 'I will leave you to yourselves; and it is not too late for me to call at the Rectory, and ask after Mrs. Trelawney.'

'You sit still,' said Mrs. Woodfall. 'Why should you hurry away for Paul? He may have some news for you too.'

'I suppose I have, in a way,' said Lawford; and Peril noticed, now that he was quieter and had become grave, that he looked, like Katty, a little haggard and a good deal tired. 'You are very kind to give me such a welcome, Katty,' he added; 'but though I'm delighted to see you, I should have been better pleased to put the meeting off a little longer. You ask if I have got a holiday—as long a one as I like to take, my dear, for Mr. Hankinson told me he was going to reduce the number of his clerks, and naturally would give the preference to those who had been with them longest.'

'Oh, Paul!' said Katty, in a deep voice of great disappointment, while Peril interjected a quick little—

'Oh, how did he dare, without consulting me—or anyone!'

Paul laughed a little. 'He is the master, you see. It would not have been very agreeable to linger on, feeling that there was nothing to do. I made my bow with the best grace I could, and came away. And besides, now that Nowell has gone, it would have been altogether a little more than I could stand.'

'Has Hugh gone, Mr. Lawford?' asked Peril, with sudden vehemence, as she leaned forward, and clasping her hands, looked earnestly into his face.

It was dusk—nearly dark, but a flickering flame from the fire cast its light upon her countenance, and it seemed to Paul that there was something almost stern in its set gravity and resolution.

'Yes, he has gone; he set sail the day before yesterday, and I went down to Liverpool to see him off. He went away in very good spirits; in better spirits than he left poor Miss Hankinson. I went to see her yesterday, and told her all about it. You don't know her much, Miss Nowell, I think?'

'Very little.'

'Well, my conviction is, that she is a really noble, unselfish woman—a little bit too unselfish, I'm afraid. If she had made rather more of an outcry, and refused to give Master Hugh her promise to wait for him, he might perhaps have acted more sensibly.'

Perhaps,' said Peril, very quietly. ' But
there are many ways of bringing people to
their senses.'

Lawford did not volunteer any more in-
formation about Hugh; Peril asked no more
questions. He was surprised to see the
apparent apathy and indifference with which
she treated the matter. He knew nothing of
the letter she had written to Nowell, or he
would perhaps have understood better the
feeling covered by this outside indifference.
As it was, he began to wonder if, perhaps,
she was coming to look at things in a less
morbid light—more healthily—less sentiment-
ally and romantically. They had been left
by Katty during this conversation. She had
remembered that Paul would be fasting and
hungry, and had slipped out to see after some
kind of a meal, and to look to the preparation
of a room for him. He sat in the chair on
which he had placed himself when he came

in, with Humphrey in his arms, and the little boy had become very quiet.

'He's gone to sleep,' observed Paul softly, looking down to the child's face.

'No wonder,' said Peril. 'He has been almost unceasingly on his feet since about ten o'clock this morning.'

'Do you care for children?'

'I never knew any properly before. I care for him. He is a very dear little boy.'

Lawford made no answer, but looked into his son's face again, and again the light flickered up. Peril saw the look—saw the changed expression; she had never seen Lawford look like that before. A deep sigh rose up in her breast—a sigh which, if she had given room to it, would have been a sob; but she repressed it.

And then Katty came in, with candles in her hand, followed by Anna with a tray, and Paul was desired to refresh himself, while the sleeping Humphrey was roused sufficiently to give a half-unconscious kiss, and stumble up the steep old stairs to bed.

It was late in the evening by the time Paul had finished his meal, and Peril, who had been silent, and had pondered over his news, felt that she wanted solitude, and must go. She rose, more decidedly this time, and went upstairs to put on her things. When she came down, Lawford stood waiting with his hat in his hand.

'I am going to walk home with you,' he said.

Peril kissed Katty silently. How was it, why should it be, that this sudden return of Paul Lawford should seem a great event, not only to these his nearest and—let us presume—dearest, but to her, a stranger and an alien, who could have no concern with him?

'You say,' she observed, as they walked

slowly down the dark lane, 'that Hugh went off in good spirits?'

'Excellent spirits. I think it was quite natural. You see, he is five-and-twenty, and strong, and full of life and hope. He has everything before him, and he is doing something which he, at any rate, thinks uncommon and very fine.'

'You don't, I suppose?' she said, a little deprecatingly.

'I do not, Miss Nowell, and I told him so. I said if he had been alone in the world, it would have been different; and so it would. He did not seem to understand that he was not alone in the world, and so he has gone.'

'I hope no harm will come to him.'

'You are very good, I am sure. I think, I must say, that he is a young man who will discover the knack of falling on his feet, wherever he is tumbled and tossed.'

'Oh, that sounds ill-natured.'

'It isn't meant so, I assure you.'

'And you, Mr. Lawford? Pardon my
question : will you stay here now, or——'

'You are very kind to take any interest in
me. I have decided upon nothing. Probably
I shall communicate with my brother-in-law
—Woodfall—and we shall have a family con-
sultation as to what is best to be done. I
really think he and I could not do better
than follow Nowell's example ; qualify ourselves to be skilled artisans, and be off to the
backwoods. It would save us many a pang,
and spare my lad heaps of mortifications
when he grows old enough to find that he is
so much poorer than other boys. Unfortu-
nately we have both a prejudice in favour of
society and civilization ; it is doubtless selfish
on our part. For the immediate present, however, I shall stay here, and give Humphrey
some lessons. Here we are at the gate of
Stanesacre House.'

'So we are! The way has been short. Good-night, Mr. Lawford. I thank you for your escort.'

He murmured some words of politeness, saw that she opened the door and entered the lighted hall, and then he turned, and took his way back towards the Grange. 'Fallen house of fallen fortunes,' he said to himself, and thought with some bitterness what an unlucky dog he was.

The front-door of his house still stood open; he went in, closing it after him, and found Katty in the parlour, seemingly very tired, for she had stretched herself upon the old sofa, and lay with her hands folded and her eyes closed. Paul stooped over her and kissed her cheek, and she opened her eyes. He saw that they were wet, and he kissed them too.

'Have you been wasting your thoughts and your tears on me, Katty?'

'Spending them, not wasting,' said she tenderly. 'I don't suppose the day will ever come when I shall consider a thought bestowed upon you wasted; at least, I hope not. Oh, Paul, forgive my carelessness tonight! I was so overjoyed to see you that I quite forgot it must have been some mishap that had brought you here so suddenly. I could have bitten my tongue out after I had asked you that question, and found that you had been sent away by that horrid man; and with Peril Nowell here, too! It was most indiscreet of me!'

'If you never commit any worse indiscretion, my dear, than that, you will do,' he said, laughing gently, as he seated himself on a chair beside her. 'Miss Nowell is quite welcome to know all about my concerns. They are so far off hers, and so far removed from all personal contact with her affairs, that it no more affects me for her to know them than it would if I heard that some one had mentioned to the Queen that I was very badly off; I mean, practically it is all the same. Fancy if the Queen tried to concern herself about every clerk who had a grievance! Fancy Peril Nowell intervening every time that her manager made a slight alteration in his business arrangements!'

'Ah!' said Katty, after a pause of reflection. 'That is all very well, Paul, to talk about the Queen—and all that. Peril is a friend—a personal friend of mine now.'

'So much the more reason why she should know all about us. I assure you, Katty, there was no sting to me in what you said. We spoke of it as I took her home. It leaves me freer than I might have been in regard to her. No one can possibly suspect any danger from *me ;* whereas, in a place like this, had I been just a little better off——'

'Oh, I know what you mean! Mrs.

Trelawney has formed Peril's future—has chosen a husband for her, and means her to marry him. Let us not talk of that; let us talk of you and of us. I sometimes wish that we were just a little better off, Paul. I wish that life were not such a hand-to-hand battle with poverty, and struggle with the wolf—if only the wolf would sometimes go away for a little while—just a little while. I get so tired of it sometimes, and feel as if I could hold out no longer.'

'You are the bravest woman, and the best, in the world,' he said, kissing her hands eagerly. 'Do not think I don't know it. What would have become of me—where would Philip have been, if it had not been for you, Katty? You said in a letter the other day that you had grown into a hag, and had not an atom of flesh on your bones. You added, I believe——'

'Wrinkles and grey hairs,' said Mrs. Woodfall prosaically; and then, with a sigh, 'and I used to be such a good-looking girl. Even you must be able to remember, Paul——'

'I remember,' said he, his voice deepening. 'I remember you when I was a boy of twelve, and you were fifteen; and how proud I was of you, Katty. A few years later when Woodfall—do you remember?—was moonstruck and helplessly in love with you. You were more than good-looking then. I never remember a lighter grace in a girl's form, or a brighter eye, or a more winning face; and, as you say, here are hollows'—and he touched her cheek—'and wrinkles'—passing his hand across her brow—'and grey hairs, one or two, to be discovered by a careful and microscopic investigation'—his hand swept gently over the still thick and glossy hair, in which here and there a grey line did appear. 'I grant you them all, my dear, since you are so eager for them; and you are more beau-

tiful with them, to me, than you were without them, Katty, my sister.'

It was with as much reverence as love that
he kissed the brow that carried the lines they
had spoken of; and Katharine was weeping
now real tears—tears which had as much of
joy as of sorrow in them.

'After all,' she said, 'we have a roof, and
we cannot starve; and—and—I wouldn't
change my husband and my brother for any
others in the world!'

'Though they have given you as much
trouble as if they had been boys instead of
men.'

'And as much delight as if they were—
what they are—perfect after their kind,' she
said, stifling a laugh which broke through her
tears. 'Oh, I do feel so much better now!
I think I must have had what a sentimental
German governess, who once boarded with
me, used to call a *dumpfe Ahnung* that you

were coming, Paolo, or that something was going to happen. I felt hysterical all day, half-inclined to cry. I had just begun in listening to Peril singing " Mignon " when you came. Now I've had it out. A nice sentimental pair we are! Let us write a letter to Philip, and just tell him how happy we are.'

She jumped off the sofa to find her writing-things, and observed, as she came to the table:

'I like Peril Nowell, Paul. I dare say there may be something wild in her; but there is something very sweet as well, to me, even in her majestic gravity. I don't wonder you were smitten with her. You know, in your first letter about her, you did rave " pretty considerably," sir.'

'Did I ?' said Paul.

'Yes, indeed! Lately there has been less about her; but, perhaps'—she spoke slowly —'not because you have thought less, eh ?'

She put her arm over his shoulder and laughed.

'No,' said her brother quietly; 'the very reverse.'

'Poor Paul!' said Katty caressingly; and they spoke not another word on the subject.

The letter to Philip was written, and then Katty, wearied with her long day's work, went to bed. Her brother sat in his dim little parlour wide awake doing nothing— pondering seemingly — until far into the night.

CHAPTER XI.

THE SPINNING OF THE WEB.

THE autumn days slipped by, until stately September had departed, and gusty October, with surging seas, and battling winds, and rack-strewed skies, was ushered in. And during these days the heart which was most unquiet in that little circle at Wiswell was, perhaps, that of Mrs. Trelawney. She had so set her heart upon carrying through her scheme, had so built upon it, and resolved upon it, that obstacles of any kind appeared very wicked to her; and when Paul Lawford appeared upon the scene, handsome, clever, and a gentleman, despite all his poverty—and, to use her own expression, 'one of those odious " old friends " who are the most dangerous people in the world when they get their chance '— when this figure came and trod the little stage on which she had placed her interesting drama, and thrust himself in, as it seemed to her, in a quite unnecessary and wholly obtrusive manner, her imagination took fire, and she foresaw all sorts of disagreeable conclusions to her play, which was to turn out so properly and so delightfully.

Peril's intimacy with that broken-down family at the Grange increased every day, as Mrs. Trelawney saw with intense uneasiness —an uneasiness which was the more harassing in that she dared not allow the faintest sign of it to appear. The only course open to her was, as she very plainly saw, to keep perfectly quiet, and speak of everything as if it were a matter of course, and get the young

lady, as soon as might be, removed from the
sphere of the obnoxious influence. Pending
this consummation she was forced to see that
her own favourite entertainments were somewhat neglected. Peril appeared seldomer on
the tennis-lawn in an afternoon ; while she
was very often away with Katty, and
Humphrey, and that horrid brother, for
whole days together, on some excursion on
shore or inland. It was true she never failed
in her attention to Mrs. Trelawney : she was
willing and eager to come to her whenever
she was asked—would sit with her, read to
her, write for her, talk to her, as much as she
pleased ; but—there were these other people
in the background, of whom she spoke always
in terms implying the most perfect equality,
citing their friendship as one of the pleasures
and benefits of her life.

‘ Just as if they were doing the favour by
letting her be with them !’ Mrs. Trelawney

said with irritation to her husband one day,
to whom she had been confiding some of her
fears and hopes—fears lest Peril should be
unduly influenced by people whose standing
was so far beneath that which would sometime be hers ; hopes that she—Mrs. Charles
Trelawney—would be successful in persuad-
ing the young heiress to join them in their
winter tour, which was now definitely settled,
Mr. Trelawney having arranged with a
fellow-clergyman to take his duty while he
was away.

'My dear,' said he quietly, 'I think you
exaggerate the mischief; but whatever may
be its extent, it is done.'

'Done !' she echoed breathlessly; 'what do
you mean ?   Has that man——'

'Maud, you go rather too far,' he said very
gravely.   'What reason have you to suppose
that young Lawford would so far forget what
is his duty as a gentleman as to attempt any

designs upon Peril Nowell and her money?
He is far too proud and fastidious, let me tell
you. I have never seen the faintest sign on
either side of anything of the kind, and I
have seen them together pretty often. As
for Mrs. Woodfall, I think her head has other
things to engage it than any such stupid
project.'

'What on earth do you mean, then, by
saying the mischief is done?' asked his wife,
not heeding the severity of his tone.

'I simply mean that she considers these
people her friends; and, with her, friendship is
friendship. Whatever becomes of her, and
whomsoever she marries or does not marry,
she will never drop them. You seem to hate
the alliance altogether so much. I merely
wished to imply that it is there, and I don't
see what gives you any right or reason to
fight against it.'

'You frightened me out of my wits. Of

course I know that; but you are so easy-going, you don't see the dangers. A man like that is just the sort of fellow to fascinate a girl like Peril Nowell. He is poor, and not afraid to confess his poverty, so that he uses it as a means of making himself interesting, instead of——'

' Uses it as a means ? You still keep harping on that string as if he had designs on poor Peril. You never were more mistaken in your life.'

' I hope I may be,' she said, inwardly more convinced than ever that he had those designs, and possessed also formidable advantages in the way of carrying them out.

Peril, meantime, was a constant guest at the Grange; while the Grange, in a body, was not unfrequently seen at Stanesacre. Mr. Wistar was overjoyed with little Humphrey. The means by which the boy had first gained his approval were as follows :

'My lad,' said Mr. Wistar, 'would you like a sixpence—to earn it, I mean?'

'Yes,' said Humphrey. 'I've got one; if I got another I could buy that boat that I saw in the toy-shop at Foulhaven.'

'Very good. Then answer me this question rightly, and the sixpence is yours. There's a place in Yorkshire—which is full of fine places, you must know—there's one small place in it called Arkingarthdale; and there's a peculiarity about it—so all the people say. There's a road into it, but no road out of it. Now, how would you get out if you had once got in, seeing that there's no road?'

'I should go back the same way,' said Humphrey, almost contemptuously.

'Bravo!' chuckled Mr. Wistar, enraptured. 'Many a bairn have I seen puzzling over that mystery; and he's cracked the nut straight away. You should have had three guesses;

but since you've found out first thing, I think it deserves a shilling instead of sixpence.'

Ever after, Humphrey had been the model of a 'sharp, fine lad' in Mr. Wistar's opinion; and if he considered the sharp lad's father to be less brilliantly endowed than the son, he nevertheless took kindly enough to Paul, while Mrs. Woodfall he considered to be a noble woman, and said so without more ado.

The intimacy deepened; but it was chiefly between Katty and Peril. She and Paul were on friendly terms—friendly enough and intimate enough to allow of an occasional dispute—she being all for impulsive measures and active work in life ; wanting to storm the citadel of success, and holding that a man should be above all things ambitious. He, who, whatever ambitions he might have had, had seen most of them pretty well levelled with the dust, but not choosing to open his heart to her, and speak to her of his disappointments or rebuffs in life, combating her with a pretended indifference to ambition and success, and a feigned love for a quiet and unobtrusive poverty, which often elicited sharp replies from her—replies which must have been rather hard for him to bear, but which he took with an unruffled calm and politeness, and an occasional gentle satire, which she was then far from appreciating. He gave a good deal of his time to Humphrey's education ; and Peril was forced to own that, however unsuccessful he might be as a votary of ambition, or an aspirant after riches, he was able to do what many a man fails in who has snatched from the world every material advantage it has to give—he could awaken and keep alive a passion of devotion and love in a childish heart like this ; he could be to his boy not only father, master, and guide, but companion, friend, and playfellow.

But, whether it was his doing or hers, the

intimacy did not grow very deep between
them. Nothing could exceed Paul's politeness to her, or hers to him, as a rule; but
she had always a secret feeling akin to contempt for him—a sort of idea that he was
harmless and useless, and that it would have
better beseemed him to go out and seek some
work than to linger on at Wiswell, acting as
tutor to his little boy, bringing him up with
ideas of refinement, and with 'the tastes of a
gentleman,' as the phrase has it, and making
no preparation to meet those tastes when the
time should come in which they would take a
more active shape. Katty ought to have
been the man, Peril said to herself. So
strong, so cheery, so brave was she, looking
her fate so unflinchingly in the face, and
ready to work at whatever her hand should
find to do.

At last came the time for making a
decision—was she going with the Trelawneys

or not? They meant to depart within a week. Peril pondered it, and said she would go. Mrs. Trelawney said very little about it, but her relief was deep and intense. She foresaw now nothing but a successful and triumphant issue to all her schemes. It was nearly the end of October; and winter in that bleak Yorkshire village was already striding rapidly nearer—twice, already, the fields had been hoar with snow, and the ponds and gutters crisp with a thin crackling ice—when the three set off. They were to be away for four or five months.

* * * * *

And during these months Mrs. Trelawney's hopes rose, and everything seemed to be working in the direction she wished for. They were joined by Stephen Harkland in Rome, whither they made their way first, and he continued their companion for the remainder of the tour. Peril seldom mentioned the Woodfall and Lawford alliance. Mrs. Trelawney began to think and hope that she was forgetting it in all the new life and the beautiful things which were a revelation for her, and which evidently made so deep an impression on her receptive mind. The only thing about it all which Mrs. Trelawney did not like was the desire for solitude, and the love of wandering off alone if she got the opportunity, and dreaming away the time in some church, or picture-gallery, or shady villa garden. She did not display any irritation when she was interrupted in these pastimes ; she seemed to have become much gentler and less vehement even since they had left home, but to the end of their tour it remained a habit of hers, and her favourite one. Perhaps Mr. Trelawney could have explained, better than his wife, the processes which were going on in the girl's mind. It is certain that he would have comprehended them, and sympathized with them, while in her they would simply have aroused wonder and irritation.

As a matter of fact, one grand idea had soon dawned upon Peril's mind, in this country, new to her, old in reality, and filled with its numberless records of a great spiritual citadel and battle-ground. *Renunciation* was the idea, the word, the thought, which assailed her and pursued her wherever she went, enrapturing her with its vastness, attracting her by its sadness, putting hope into her by the glorious promise it held out of peace, of contentment, and of rest, to those who obeyed it. Of course it was working in her towards developments which neither she nor anyone else could foresee—developments as likely to be grotesque as grand; but it was there, a powerful leaven, an influence stronger than any spiritual one she had ever felt yet. The glorious idea that, by a simple, consistent course of action in one direction—so plain and clear that a child could follow it—one might gain a victory, complete and irrefutable, over the world, the flesh, and the devil, all three of which had been grievous tormentors to her ; could get a guide which should be infallible, a light which should be the same for highest and lowest ; should get peace—this thought made her tremble and thrill whenever it entered her heart. And it seemed to be everywhere ; strange spiritual experiences tinctured every day of those which she passed under Italian skies, in Italian cities. Everywhere she saw this same solemn lesson of renunciation enforced ; she saw it in the long processions of monks, and in the gliding figures of veiled nuns as they noiselessly passed her ; it spoke to her, low as a whisper, yet loud as thunder, from the pale lips of the Christs who hung suspended from the dim walls of great cathedrals ; or elevated, glow-

ing on canvases tinted by master-hands, above
the high altars, with tapers for ever glimmering before them, as if to emphasize the lesson
with fire.   Before these images she saw men
and women kneel ; and it seemed to her that,
if she had been able to kneel also, with faith,
her problem would be solved.   Daily, in her
own room, she pored over the words of the
Gospel, which seemed to illuminate and be
illuminated by this new discovery of hers,
and over old Thomas à Kempis ; and what
she studied worked potently in her towards
results of a bizarre nature enough ; for she
had got the idea, and, as was natural enough,
began to apply it concretely, and not spiritu-
ally or abstractly.   Her impulse was to do
something—make some great sacrifice—and
then it seemed as if the spiritual results, the
peace, the calm, the inward fulness and contentment, would follow.   Even in worldly
things—in plays and dramas—it seemed to

follow her and cry aloud to her. She had
been taking lessons in German and Italian,
and was very naturally more attracted by the
former. With her usual love of plunging
into the heart of things at once—picking the
choicest plums at the first handful—she pur-
chased a copy of Goethe's ' Faust' as soon as
she knew a few words and phrases of the
language, and a word-for-word translation of
the same ; and, before long, came upon the
immortal, if hackneyed, passage, which was
as fresh, as new, as miraculous to her as if it
had first been uttered yesterday :

> ' In jedem Kleide werd' ich wohl die Pein
> Des engen Erdelebens fühlen.
> Ich bin zu alt um nur zu spielen,
> Zu jung um ohne Wunsch zu sein.
> Was kann die Welt mir wohl gewähren ?
> *Entbehren sollst du, sollst entbehren !*'

She read, she felt, she thought she understood. How could it be that she did not
understand, when every word went home to

her with such force, like a blow—as if some stranger had pulled out the secrets of her heart, and showed them to her?

Absorbed in this new hope and promise of new life, she rushed into the path she had found with an eagerness which was in itself a kind of selfishness—the passionate desire of youth to escape from its sufferings, to get away from the oppression it feels, to annihilate the burden by some great and effective sudden action, rather than to bow the neck and stoop the back, and plod on under it, until years and patience have made its weight bearable, and even acceptable as ballast.

46—2

CHAPTER XII.

DUST AND ASHES.

'OH, Peril, you *have* disappointed me!'

'I am very sorry if I have, Mrs. Trelawney; but I do not see why you should be disappointed; at least, I do not see what right you have to be disappointed in this thing.'

Peril, exceeding pale, with dilated eyes and fluttering nostril, looked straight into the face of Mrs. Trelawney, from whom extreme mortification and irritation combined had wrung the first words. Never had the girl addressed her in such a manner before—

never so looked at her—with angry eyes and form rigid with temper. Mrs. Trelawney felt a thrill, in spite of herself. Peril's 'temper,' of which she had heard so much from Peril herself, had slumbered ever since she knew her; she had never once seen it; but here it was at last, roused and erect. Mrs. Trelawney had the vexation of feeling that she had not exorcised the evil spirit; it had been soothed, dormant; but it lived, and could turn upon even her.

They were back at Wiswell. The time of the year was April. They had already been home three weeks. A week ago, Stephen Harkland, whom they had left in Paris, had also returned. On the previous afternoon he had ridden over to Stanesacre, having at last broken loose from Mrs. Trelawney's warnings and cautions, which he began to find irksome. He had found Peril in, and had asked her to be his wife; had told her that he knew all the conditions which bound her, and, if she would only take him, he was ready to do as she wished—wait out the appointed time for her, or marry her to-morrow, and forfeit her great fortune.

'My father consents, and I have enough, and more than enough, if you will only take me along with it, Peril.'

It was a generous, unworldly, uncalculating offer, as she in her seclusion, and with even her want of knowledge of the world, had sense enough to know; and Peril had been moved to tears, as she sorrowfully but most decidedly refused it. And when he asked her why, she told him that she would not do him so great a wrong as to marry him; she did not love him, and she had other things to think of than marriage at present. There had been a brief, low-voiced conversation. Was she absolutely certain? Would she never by any chance change her mind?

Would she not leave a chance open to him if he were to come again in a year, or two years? She shook her head, brokenly but somehow indubitably managed to convey to him that it would never be of any use for him to come again; and Stephen, saying dismally, 'Then I might as well set off on my travels again,' had taken his leave, and ridden away, and Peril had sat down and cried heartily, just as any other girl might do who has had to give pain to a man whom she likes and wishes well to, but whom she would on no account take as her life's companion. It did not occur to her that Stephen would speak to anyone else—then, at any rate—of his disappointment; and she had come to-day to the Rectory, unknowing that Mrs. Trelawney was acquainted with what had passed, and not meaning to say anything about it. She was received coolly, distantly, frostily, and as she said some commonplace words, Mrs. Trelawney had broken in, in an icy voice, with the words :

'Stephen Harkland came to see me yesterday afternoon.'

Peril flushed up, and said merely, ' Did he?'

And then followed the two harder blows, recorded at the beginning of the chapter.

Mrs. Trelawney was exasperated beyond what words could tell, at this failure of her scheme.   She had condoled with Stephen, but had felt fit at the same time to box his ears.   She felt that she must now use some finesse if she wished to prevent an explosion on Peril's part; but her impulse was to tell her that she was a presumptuous chit, and wanted whipping for taking upon herself to refuse the position of Mrs. Stephen Harkland.

Indeed, this was what Mrs. Trelawney very strongly felt.   With all her real affection for Peril, and her profound interest, she had

never been able quite to forget that she herself was an aristocrat, and that Peril Nowell
sprang on both sides from the people; on
her mother's side from small yeomanry; on
that of her father, from—there was no dis-
guising it—a plain, undeniable Lancashire
operative. If Peril had followed her dictates,
this difference would have been so beautifully,
so perfectly varnished over, that no one would
have perceived it; as it was, the rift became
very visible to Mrs. Trelawney, at any rate.
Whatever Peril felt, the rector's wife had a
strong consciousness that she was a superior
being who had taken the girl by the hand,
and given her advantages, by the mere asso-
ciation with her and hers, which all her wealth
could never have procured for her. And
then her *protégée* turned upon her, and told
her she had no right to be disappointed in
what she had done. Said it, too, with crest
erect and flashing eyes, and a look of breath-

less passion about her, which made Mrs. Trelawney shrink in dismay at the idea of the gulf there was beneath—of the scene that might take place, if she gave way to the feelings that possessed her.

'In my ignorance,' she said, choking down a feeling of burning anger, 'I encouraged the poor boy by every means in my power to seek your society. I imagined that a union with him would have solved all your difficulties.'

'I think it was a pity to encourage him, and say nothing to me about it. If you had explained yourself to me, I could have told you at once that it was out of the question.'

This was so exasperatingly true, that Mrs. Trelawney felt herself more injured than ever.

'Surely you could see,' she said. 'Did you never ask yourself why he followed us, and stayed with us as he did?'

'Never,' said Peril composedly. 'I was not thinking about him. I was thinking of other things altogether. It made no difference to me whether he came or went—whether he was there or not. And I should think either of you might have seen that.'

True again, and Mrs. Trelawney had seen it in her heart of hearts, and had refused to accept the sign.

'A child might have seen that he was in love with you. And as for you—I don't know. You seemed to live in a dream—you were always wandering away to places, and liked best to be alone, and——'

'So I was *in love*, of course!' said Peril, with unutterable contempt. 'Can one be thinking of nothing but a man, when one wishes for solitude? If that is what you believe, I suppose you would only laugh to hear that I was thinking of religion, and of a holy life, and was trying, while I was far

away from my troubles, to learn how I should
act when I grew a little older, and became
responsible for what I did—legally, I mean.
Mr. Trelawney would understand—he would
know what I mean when I say that I was
trying to be better—that I was fighting the
devils which have always been ready to
overthrow me.   I was not thinking of Stephen
Harkland, or feeling in love with him.   How
can you imagine such a thing ?'

Her voice swelled with tears of indignation.

' I imagined and hoped that you were
growing less morbid, and more like other
ordinary, healthy young women,' said Mrs.
Trelawney tartly.   ' And I find that instead,
the very reverse was taking place.'

' You have been very good to me,' said
Peril, with the same still, but concentrated
passion in her dark glance, 'and I shall be
grateful to you all my life ; but I do not
understand that that gives you the right to

tell me how I shall think, or when my thoughts are morbid, or even to say whom I shall marry. You are not me—you have not lived what I have—you are not like me, and you cannot tell what is good for me.'

'I cannot carry on a discussion of this kind,' said Mrs. Trelawney, almost beside herself with mingled anger and mortification.

Every one of Peril's words went home to her. She became conscious that she had taken far too much upon herself—had wished to interfere far too arbitrarily in another person's life—and the knowledge that her motives had been so unimpeachable, and that yet they did not justify her interference, added bitterness to the gall. She had begun to flatter herself that Peril Nowell, whatever she might be with others, was docile with her. She learnt her mistake in an overwhelming manner. She did not know the extraordinary restraint which the girl was

now putting on herself—she did not know
the mildness of this outbreak compared with
former ones; but she felt it altogether un-
bearable, such as it was.

'I cannot go on with it,' she repeated,
drawing in her breath. 'I am sorry to seem
ungracious, but this has upset me so terribly
that I must ask you to leave me. I must
not see you for a time. I——'

'You tell me to go,' said Peril, her face
now very white indeed. 'I shall go, Mrs.
Trelawney. But I must say one thing before
I go. I feel that I am in the right in this;
therefore, if ever you want to see me again,
it is you who must send for me—and I will
come, gladly—but I shall not seek you. And
I want to say, too, that I thought you were
so kind to me because you cared for me—a
little bit. But I find it was because you
wished me to marry Mr. Harkland, who I
know is your old friend, and like a son to

you. I might have known that no one would love me very much for myself—I am too unhappy and too ill-tempered—but it is the same grief to me as if I had not known. Good-bye!'

Mrs. Trelawney could not stop her—she was not prepared to apologize, though she knew she ought to do so. The girl's name, which she tried to call, seemed to stick fast in her throat. She had just one glimpse of a beautiful face, pale, and more sorrowful now than wrathful, when those great scintillating dry eyes were withdrawn, the flutter of a skirt, the closing of the door—and silence.

Anger, mortification, disgust, all struggled violently within her, till she muttered at last:

'It is what I might have expected. There is no breeding—no blood—no race in her. It is a lucky escape for Stephen, and a warning to me, by which I will profit. I will never make a friend again. Termagant that she is !'

And then, when the fires of anger and passion died down, she began to recall certain words of Peril's—certain tones which pierced her heart when she thought of them. 'I might have known that no one would love me for my own sake—you wanted me to marry Mr. Harkland.' She had gone away with that impression, and Mrs. Trelawney, whose mind was logical enough when she chose to let it be so, felt that indeed Peril had cause enough for saying what she did about her.

The afternoon seemed very long; it was later than usual when her husband came in, looking very grave, even stern. She saw the darkness on his brow, and quailed. He would tell her the truth, as Peril had done.

'Maud,' he began, almost instantly, ' I have met Peril Nowell, and it seems to me that you have gone the way to embitter her against her lot more than ever.'

'Spare me Peril Nowell and her tempers!' she rejoined, with acerbity.

From the look in her husband's eye, she read the comment that it was not Peril Nowell alone who was afflicted with a temper.

'She has disappointed me cruelly,' she observed.

'And it seems to me that you have meddled most unwarrantably in her concerns. My dear child, what in heaven above, or in the earth beneath, gives you authority to say whom she shall marry, or whom she shall not marry? And to upbraid her for refusing a young fellow for whom she cares not a straw—why, the world is turning upside down. The poor girl has complications enough in her life— why she should add to them by taking a husband whom she doesn't want, is really past my comprehension.'

This was a hideously commonplace way of putting it.

'I wish to hear no more about her,' she repeated.

Mr. Trelawney knew when, as the vulgar saying hath it, 'to let well alone;' he gathered from the brevity of his wife's replies that she had found out her mistake, if she had not got to the point of owning it. He merely said :

'I certainly have no wish to discuss the matter, but it grieves me to the heart to think that she should have any justification for thinking that she was encouraged to come here, not as a friend, but as an aspirant for Stephen Harkland's hand.'

Then he was silent, and if there was a mortified soul in England that night, it inhabited the earthly tenement of Maud Trelawney.

PART III.

THE CUTTING OF THE KNOT.

CHAPTER I.

HOW THE ORACLE SPOKE.

PERIL, on the following evening, found her way to the Grange. Mr. Wistar, who had gone to Foulhaven, had said he might call for her there on his way back.

The door stood open, and there was an unusual silence over the house. Peril entered the hall, and listened for a moment. From the 'sitting-room,' as it was called, came voices—that of Paul persuasively:

'And what was the next thing that this bad king did?'

'Oh,' said Humphrey, in an off-hand

manner, 'he wanted to make slaves of his
people, so he——'

Slightly smiling, Peril turned into the other
room, where she found Katty seated in the
window, industriously laying the last tints
upon a water-colour drawing. There was a
look of work about her. It was not the
dabbling of an amateur who works in a per-
functory manner to amuse himself; and this
was what Peril felt, with something like a pang,
every time she saw Katty's absorbed stooping
over her work.

She looked up, and her bright smile flashed
across her worn face!

'Oh, Peril, I'm glad to see you! You
have not shown yourself for a long time now.'

'If I interrupt you, tell me so, and I will be
as quiet as a mouse till you have done.'

'But you don't. I have just finished.'

'Are you going to send that away soon ?'

'Yes. I wish I could make out whether

this man is dealing fairly with me or not. He sent me a condescending announcement that he had "succeeded in disposing of my last sketches," and if I liked would try to do the same by some more. Now it is a very short time since I sent him my last, and it seems to me——'

'Write to him and tell him that you want more money for your pictures. I would. And that if he doesn't give you more you will sell them to some one else.'

'And perhaps hear immediately that since I was not satisfied with the terms he made for me, perhaps we had better cease to do any business together. Peril, my dear, I hope you may never know what it is to want money very badly, and be afraid to throw away your one little chance, though you have an indignant feeling all the time that you are being defrauded.'

'I hope *you* may never know what it is to

have more money than you want, or care for,
or can possibly dispose of, thrust upon you
against your will, while—Katty, I would
think your poverty the height of bliss
compared with my riches.   And you wouldn't
exchange with me—you know you would
not.'

'Everyone prefers his own, just because it
is his own, not because it is the best,' said
Katty evasively.

'Me, for instance,' said Peril, with a little
hard laugh.   'I wish a lot of things could be
annihilated.'

'Such as ?'

'Such as the law which makes it impossible
for me to come to you, and say, " See, I am
all alone, with so much money ; I will cast in
my lot with yours, and we will make common
cause together."   How happy I should be,
and yet——'

'My dear, I sometimes think those rules

are very absurd too; but for goodness' sake don't let Paul hear you say such a thing !'

' I don't mean to,' said Peril. ' I know very well what he would do, if I did ; begin to talk in the politest way, and gradually flay one alive with ridicule and a sort of amused contempt. I heard him instructing Humphrey about the wickedness of a king, as I came in. Humphrey seemed alive to the enormity of the thing.'

' I think he gives Humphrey too many lessons. It takes him out of himself, of course; and he is troubled enough now, though he would never show it.'

' Is he ? Why ? At least, if I may ask why ?'

' Oh, certainly. We haven't got any secrets. My poor, good husband thinks he won't be able to keep his present place very long—and then farewell to this pleasant loitering life here. We must begin to think of something else ; and I think—Paul thinks—I believe we shall have to—sell the Grange.'

' Sell the Grange—and not live here any more ?'

' We could not *very* well live here, if we sold it,' said Mrs. Woodfall drily.

' And go away from Wiswell ?'

' Probably to one of the colonies, like your respected cousin, Mr. Hugh Nowell. There we might begin a new life altogether, without any shams : work with our hands and earn our living in the sweat of our brows, and do our duty in *that* state of life, you know. Also, if we do decide upon anything of this kind, it will have to be soon, before Humphrey grows older ; while he is young enough to take to the roughing it, and get to feel kindly towards a backwoodsman's life.'

' You are joking,' said Peril, in a low voice. ' You do not really mean it.'

' I mean it in very solemn earnest.'

'What *will* become of me, if you go!' was wrung from Peril by the prospect.

'Return to your first allegiance to Mrs. Trelawney, who will be very glad to know you removed from the influence of such shabby-genteel, undistinguished people as we are.'

Peril did not enter into facts as to her quarrel with Mrs. Trelawney, but she began to realize that she would be left with a prospect of solitude and dreariness which it appalled her to contemplate. With the knowledge that Hugh Nowell was gone; estranged from Mrs. Trelawney; the Lawfords and Woodfalls coming to the decision that they had better dispose of their property and leave the country—what would she do—how support her weary, lonely, embittered existence? Her troubles, so many a one would have told her, were of her own making. Perhaps they were so, in great measure; and yet I think not wholly so, nor was it wholly possible for her to have escaped them. If her temper was violent and her anger wild, so also was her remorse deep, and her struggles passionate after a happier and better state of things. She had fought, she was fighting still, to get out of the toils that herself had spun for herself, and it seemed, so far, as if the only result of her endeavours was this—that she was to be left alone, with most of the struggle to begin over again. She made no distinct answer to Katty's last remark, but said seriously :

' If you do this, how soon do you think it will be ?'

' It ought to be soon,' said Katty. ' Indeed, the sooner the better for us. When a thing of that sort is pending, it only adds to the troubles and the heartaches of it to linger. South Africa is what they talk of. Fancy us, Peril, all four of us, trying to be at home in South Africa, and thinking of this dear, damp, peaceful old place, and the Wiswell cliffs, and —everything !'

'Don't—I can't bear it !'

'Though I have lived here such a short time, comparatively, I love it, I can't tell you how much. I have been able to be at home here; to feel as if I could bear to live here always, if I had to, without any trouble or discontent; in fact, with great thankfulness. I feel,' said Katty, seating herself on the sofa beside Peril, and propping her chin upon her hand as she looked at her with her bright, large eyes, 'as if, though I am quite young yet—only thirty-four, Peril—that I have been fighting, fighting, fighting, all my life. I have never known what rest and shelter meant. If you know what I mean, I have had to be like a watchdog, sleeping with one eye open and one ear pricked up ; no rest, no oblivion—forgetfulness—no luxury of complete repose, for me. I don't complain ; I have

had things, along with these conditions, that I
would not exchange for the greatest prosperity.
If I had been very rich, perhaps I should never
have known moments such as I have known.
Perhaps, if my husband had had ten thousand
a year, he might have hired nurses to look
after me when I was ill for many weeks,
instead of nursing me himself, as—as no
woman could have done. Ah!'—Katharine
pressed her hand over her eyes to keep her
tears back—' I would not change ; and yet,
I feel somehow as if this prospect of expatria-
tion were too much for me.   I feel as if, when
we have sold the Grange and gone away,
we shall have burnt our ships, spiked our
guns, or whatever you like that is dangerous
and desperate.   And it seems as if there was
an ocean of never-ending work before me,
which I don't feel up to.   I have that awful
feeling of being—what some one once said is
the most dreadful feeling one can have—

weaker than my task.   It will pass over, I dare say.   I hope so ; but that is the feeling I have at present.'

Peril had taken her disengaged hand, and stroked it softly.

' There must be something wrong in the order of things which lets people like you be so harassed and worn, and provides so bounti-fully for useless, cumbering clods like me,' she said bitterly.

Her heart was beating, and her eyes dim. She scarce admitted to herself the idea which had begun to creep into her mind.   There was a wildness about it which seemed like madness, and a delicious fascination—the promise of fulfilment thereby of her great craving to do something real, something strong and solid, of cutting at one stroke through her difficulties, which made her tremble inwardly and secretly—as some of us perhaps know what it is to tremble, with an intuition, a revelation, an *idea*—that most blessed of things, and the one that is most rarely dispensed—she trembled then with this sacred quiver, half fear, half joy, and felt not quite sure whether to bow her head and weep, or lift up her voice and sing for joy. Perhaps it was extravagant, exaggerated, far-fetched— that may be—it was Peril.

'Ah!' Katty said, in answer to her last words, 'it's an odd world. We must take it as we find it, and not look too deeply into it, unless we want to die, or go mad.'

Just then there was a sound from the other room—a wild whoop of joy from a child's voice, and a scuffle as of chairs pushed back ; and Paul's tones in mild accents, admonishing his son.

'Thank goodness he's released the poor little thing at last,' said Katty, starting up, quite restored to her usual self. 'Peril, *at* your peril you reveal to Paul what I have said to you! He must not know. It would just put the finishing-touch to his difficulties to know that I had lost heart.'

'I have no such confidences with him as that would imply,' said Peril, with a vibration in her voice. 'If I ventured to say anything about your concerns, he would laugh at me, and institute a comparison between yours and mine, as he always does.'

Something in her tone or manner struck Katty; she looked sharply at her as if about to speak, but ere she could do so Paul had come into the room, with some noise and circumstance, caused by Humphrey's having grasped his hand, and used it as a sort of pulley whereby to swing himself round and round.

'Heyday!' remarked Lawford; 'here's a visitor!'

'Miss Nowell!' shouted Humphrey in

stentorian tones, making a rush at her, and
dashing upon her knee.

It was a rough embrace which followed
—she loved these stormy onslaughts of
Humphrey, because they were always sponta-
neous, unasked for, unconventional—dictated
by sheer goodwill and liking, not restrained
by timidity or company manners. He rushed
at her and hung upon her neck, and gave her
loud resounding kisses, with just as little
ceremony as he used towards his father and
his aunt Katty. More than once she had
returned the lad's salutes with a vigour and a
passion which she could hardly have explained, except by calling it joy in his love ;
but to-night she felt herself thrill strangely as
he dashed up to her, in all the boisterous
strength of the reaction of getting free from
his lesson, and swarmed on to her knee, un-
heeding his own roughness, and threw his
little rough serge-clothed arms round her

neck, and bestowed a smacking kiss upon her cheek.

'Come! come!' observed Lawford, seizing hold of him; 'that's enough. People don't care to be smothered by you. Good-evening, Miss Nowell.'

'Good-evening,' said she quietly, as she put her hand in his. 'Leave Humphrey alone—I like him on my knee. Tell me about that king, Humphrey, who wanted to enslave his people. Did he succeed?'

'You've been listening!' said Humphrey, with less than his usual courtesy; 'or else how could you have heard? I don't know about that king. I was so tired, and my father did tease so.'

'Fie! tease!'

'Yes, he did,' Humphrey maintained. 'He says I'm to do all my lessons now, and have no prizes.'

'Dear! dear!'

48—2

'It's a shame,' said the youth, emboldened
by what he considered his secure position on
Miss Nowell's knee; for he had noticed, without arguing anything from the fact, that when
he succeeded in getting anywhere near Peril—
on her knee, or snuggled up beside her on
the sofa-corner—he was safe from the frequent
fillips and verbal teasings of his father,
which he liked well enough, for he adored
him; but he also had a wholesome awe of
him, from which it was an agreeable relief to
escape now and then into mutinous, half-
insolent words, as now.

'It's a shame,' he repeated.

But his day of triumph was short, for his
aunt, who had caught sight of his boots,
suddenly uttered an exclamation short and
sharp.   Like lightning his guilty conscience
stung him, and caused him to draw up his feet,
and try to curl them under him in a manner
more rapid than smooth and agreeable.

'Don't kick me with your great hobnailed boots!' said his protectress, in a tone of indignant expostulation.

'I'll hobnail him!' cried Mrs. Woodfall excitedly. 'Come away this minute, sir! How dare you keep on those boots all this time, that you were in all the pools with this morning? If you don't catch your death of cold! Come upstairs and let me feel your stockings!'

He was dragged by the hand from his place of refuge, and the two whirled out of the room, with an echo in Humphrey's tones lingering behind them :

'Aunt Katty, salt water doesn't give cold. It doesn't matter a bit!' then a great clattering and clamping overhead.

Paul and Peril sat in the darkening parlour for a little while, until he said :

'Won't you give me a song in the gloaming, Miss Nowell?'

'Yes, if you like; but what do you like?'
asked Peril, getting up and going towards the
piano.

So admirably had Paul mastered and
disciplined his manner to her, that she,
though still tremulous with the idea which
had lately flashed into her mind, felt absolutely at ease with him—as much at ease
now as ever she had done. The idea
had been startling to her; but she was
convinced that to him, if ever he should
hear it, it would be a revelation—a thing
unheard of.

'Grave or gay? Light or dark?' she
continued, as he opened the piano.

'I wonder what you would say if I suggested something light and gay?' said he,
with the little smile of suppressed derision
which she knew so well—by no means un-
kindly derision, but extreme amusement and
raillery combined. 'Something *lively*,' he

pursued ; and the smile was less suppressed—
' something with tra-la-la in it.'

Peril laughed a little.

' I am sure I wish I could sing pretty
French *chansonettes*, or even English ones.
I never do care to sing to people, because
I am aware how depressing my repertory
must be. What seems to me fine and
natural is dismal to many people, I am
sure.'

' I always preferred contralto voices,' said
he ; ' and one must accept the—must I call it
penalty of such a preference—grave songs
rather than gay ones. I will have " Mignon,"
if you will give it me ; or " In questa tomba;"
or " Che farò senza Eurydice ?" or " Lascia
ch'io pianga ;" or——'

' I will sing you none of those, but a new
song that I learnt a little while ago,' said
Peril, seating herself, and striking some
chords ; and then she sang the words of the

verses that Mr. Trelawney had given her :

'Dear blossoms, roses red.'

Lawford listened : he was standing, leaning with his back against the wall by the window, and his arms folded. Peril sang well, the songs that suited her ; and it seemed to him that this suited her perfectly. The melody was a simple, sad, somewhat monotonous one —it derived its fire, its force, and its colour from the expression which she succeeded in putting into it. The last lines especially she sang with a kind of passion, of what, if it was not actually conviction, at least strove hard to be so.

'Good-bye, good-bye, good-bye,
Blue, perfect summer sky,
And all the dreams of hope and youth that wandered
Towards heaven on sun-bright wings ;
A new chant in me springs,
And gone are the old ecstasies I pondered.

Farewell, ye high designs ;
The wreath that manhood twines
Is better than the leaves youth wildly plucked and
squandered.'

Her voice trembled violently, so that it almost broke. Abruptly she stopped, playing a false note, that sent a harsh discord through the echoes.

'Truly, I have never heard that song before,' said Lawford. 'What is it? What is its name?'

'It has no name. Mr. Trelawney gave me the words.'

'And where did you find the music?'

'The music,' she repeated, with some embarrassment. 'Oh! that came—I don't know how. There is music in the words. They shape themselves into a kind of melody.'

'You composed it, I suppose you mean?' said Paul. 'I like it; but I won't ask you to sing it again just now, for I heard at the end that it was a little too much for you.'

She said nothing, but her fingers strayed softly over the keys, till at last, looking up, she saw Paul's eyes fixed upon her, his head a little bent forward, and a half-smile upon his face.

'What is the matter? Why do you look at me?' she asked hastily.

'I was only wondering whether I should tell you,' he said, in the most deliberate of tones, 'that that lad's rough caresses have unloosed all your hair at one side. I like it as it is,' he added, with no more trouble in his voice and no more significance in his look than if he had been telling Katty herself the same thing; 'but I once heard a lady stigmatize very strongly the brutality of leaving anyone in ignorance of such a thing——'

'Perhaps hers was false, and she feared it might drop off,' said Peril, with an uneasy laugh, as she felt her face flush under his deliberate, cool, and critical glance.

'Or perhaps there was some one there to whom she grudged the pleasure of the spectacle,' he suggested composedly, and watching her as she tried to gather up the heavy braids which had fallen over her shoulder. 'No; you have left a great piece of it still—here.'

He was either very indifferent, or very sure of himself, for he bent forward, and with a slight movement stretching out his hand over her stooping neck, lifted the tress of hair, and put it into the fingers that were groping for it. Their touches encountered. Peril, whose whole heart and soul were disturbed by her new speculations, felt herself start, and knew that the blood rushed in an unruly manner over her face. She did not speak; she kept her head bent down, and twisted the loosened hair into a coil. Lawford

leaned back again into his original pose as
calmly and tranquilly as if nothing had
happened.   With some little difficulty she
made the plait fast, dropped her hands upon
her lap for a moment, essayed to begin her
playing again, rose suddenly, and went back
to the dark corner of the sofa where she had
been when Paul and Humphrey had entered
the room.   She felt oppressed and breath-
less—felt faint-hearted, and shrank in terror
from the thoughts she had had half an hour
ago; and yet she felt the same thought
nearer and stronger, and more importunate
now than it had been then.

'I wonder if much damage has been done
by the wet boots,' observed Paul specula-
tively; 'because there is an ominous and portentous silence above, which I do not understand, except on the theory of his having
been sent to bed at once.'

This surmise turned out to be correct.

Directly afterwards Katty appeared ; uttered a great ' Oh dear !' and sank exhausted into a chair.

'What's the matter ?' asked her brother, going up to her.

'Oh, nothing ! It's only that child. I have such a horror of croup,' said Mrs. Woodfall ; and the little prosaic details sounded in Peril's ears like words in a dream. ' His stockings were soaking, you know—soaking ; and his feet as cold as stones. I've given him a hot bath and put him to bed ; and nothing will serve him, Peril, but for you to go upstairs and say good-night to him, if you don't mind.'

'Yes,' said Peril mechanically ; and she rose and went upstairs to the darkened room where the boy's little bed stood.

Loth though he had been to go to bed, he was now more than half asleep, and scarcely stirred when she bent over him.

'Good-night, Humphrey! Will you come and ride Bonnyface to-morrow?'

'Yes—yes,' came drowsily from him; and then, with a last gleam of struggle with his drowsiness, he put his arms round her neck, bestowed a somewhat limp and incoherent kiss upon her, and murmured, half to her and half to himself: 'I love you, Peril! God bless Miss Nowell and all my friends! I——'

He was fast asleep, and did not feel the few heavy tears that dropped from her eyes upon his fresh young face.

'Perhaps,' said Peril within herself, wiping these tears away before she went to encounter the gaze of the elders, who were not yet sleepy, 'if I can, and if—if everything were managed, you need not go to South Africa and rough it, my bonny little Humphrey!'

Mr. Wistar tarried so long in his coming—if coming he were at all—that Peril at last said she would go away if Mr. Lawford would walk with her to Stanesacre. It was odd, the manner in which she took it for granted that what had been such an unexpected illumination to her, must be as yet a hidden secret from him. If Lawford had been her elder brother she could not have treated him with more unruffled composure. But she went to bed that night feeling, for the first time in her life almost, as if a light, broad and strong, beamed from above upon her path—as if life at last held a purpose for her—its mere existence, she fancied, and its tangibility would give her strength to carry it through. The possibility of any backslidings, any variableness or shadow of turning, did not occur to her. If it occurred to youth as often as it does to maturity—or if, on its occurrence, youth treated the idea with anything other than contempt, much of the best work—most of the brightest deeds of this world—in this life would remain for ever undone.

CHAPTER II.

IN THE OLD CHURCHYARD.

T was nearly a week later—a soft, mild, grey evening at the very end of April. One might imagine the month of tears and smiles suddenly overcome with gravity, as the reflection came over her that her course was run. The wind was south-west, which on that easterly coast covered the sky with soft, fleecy grey clouds, and cast a haze over the sea and headland and cliff, and over everything to the east. A still, warm and almost sultry evening. If it had been June, one must have awaited a thunderstorm; being April, one glanced at

the grey, brooding sky, and the softened tints
on field and tree, and wondered a little how
it came to be like this. It was still broad
daylight, though daylight of this tempered,
chastened kind, when Paul Lawford strolled
up to the little wicket opening upon the little
flight of steps that led into that disused
churchyard in which Peril had wandered one
day, in the midst of which stood the deserted
church, with its weird, whirling 'tokens of
affection' suspended from the chancel-roof—
the yard which was thick with sweet cliff-
grass, and strewed with the tombs of master
mariners and first-class seamen.

In many places such a churchyard would
have been the evening resort of the village
folk—of the girls and their sweethearts, the
gossips and their cronies. But this was not
the case here. In Wiswell, all the interest
concentrated on the sea-shore, on the sloping
beach at the foot of the village where the

fishing-boats landed, where the nets were mended, and also where, less romantic to relate, the fish were turned out, counted, picked out, and disposed of without much regard to the olfactory nerve, or to sanitary conditions. Besides, Wiswell old church was deserted, and rustic folk are not fond of a deserted churchyard. The place was lonesome, solitary, and, of an evening, often unvisited for weeks together. When Lawford entered it, he found himself alone—a very brief investigation served to prove that to him—alone, and in a profound stillness, for the wind wafted the cheerful noises of the village in the opposite direction. He took his way towards the south-east corner of the church, where was a sheltered spot, completely shrouded from the view of any passers-by on the road, or indeed in the churchyard itself, unless they actually turned the corner, and came into the place itself. He looked about him, seated himself upon a low wall which divided the yard from a field, at the foot of which he could just distinguish the chimneys of Stanesacre House amongst its trees, and pulled a letter out of his pocket. He opened it, and read it, perhaps for the fiftieth time, with brows a little contracted, and pulling his moustache the while, as a man does when he is puzzled or mystified.

'DEAR MR. LAWFORD,

'Will you do me a favour? It is to be at the south-east corner of Wiswell old church to-night at eight o'clock, where I will join you. I wish to speak to you in private, for you can do me a very great kindness if you will. I beg you will not think this a strange or presumptuous request. I think I shall be able to explain myself.

'I am,
'Yours very truly,
'PERIL NOWELL.'

49—2

As he raised his eyes from looking at this signature, which meant to him—who should say what?—they fell upon the figure of Peril herself. She was dressed, whether by accident or design, in black; a loose black scarf was thrown about her shoulders, and she wore her favourite great flapping hat, with its long plume. She came gliding quickly along, with pale face, eyes that looked larger than usual, and had in them a strained, anxious expression, and slightly parted lips.

Paul rose, taking off his hat, and looking at her very gravely. He folded up her letter, and put it in his pocket.

'It was very good of you to come,' she said rather breathlessly, as she gave him her hand.

'Was it? I don't quite see why, but I would not contradict you.'

She gave a feeble, nervous smile, which died away before it had properly appeared.

Lawford felt puzzled still. This was not the Peril he knew. He had seen her moody and sad; he had seen her in anger and in bitterness; once or twice he had seen her overflowing with a sort of eerie mirth, teasing everyone around her, and saying things which stung, though they might be intended for jest. But thus—pallid, low-voiced, nervous, with wavering eyes, and lips that seemed now about to quiver into a flickering smile, now to sob bitterly—thus, he had never seen her before.

He had made various conjectures as to what she wanted him for. He had almost unhesitatingly connected the summons with her cousin Hugh, and with some plan on her part for making him take his own; perhaps she wanted him to go as a special envoy with some desperate message to the young man. This nervousness might be the result of embarrassment as to how to offer to pay his expenses, and give him a commission on the expedition; so he put it baldly and brutally to himself. For his own part, he considered her quite capable of that or any other freak; but he loved her, and her glooms and her moods—ay, and her passions and her tempers: loved the proud, untamable creature, perhaps because of her very unlikeness to himself; she took every incident of her life with such passionate, uncompromising earnestness—it was all life or death. He had gone on very well until he had known her, and then it had, to use his own phrase, been 'all up with him.' His inmost soul delighted in her beauty and the matchless loveliness of her face and form, while his spirit was fascinated by her wayward, dangerous nature. In certain moments, since he had known her, he had indulged himself in the luxury of imagining a vain thing, such as a union between them—some bond, marriage, or love,

or something that bound them together; and
one of his favourite scenes was in imagination
to rouse her into anger, or temper, or a burst
of unreasonableness, and then tame her down
to a submission, a repentance, and a humility
made piquant by the fact that they were the
outcome of such opposite tempers. She had
fascinated him—she possessed his imagination—her voice, and her look, and her eyes,
haunted him by day and by night. He had
his voice, and his manner, and his speech to
her well under control, chiefly because there
had never been any question between them
of anything but a sort of cool, intimate ac-
quaintanceship—because he felt that she did
not love him, did not suspect him of loving
her. There was no provocation, no temptation
from her; hence his calmness and composure.
And he maintained it even now, because,
judging her from what he knew of her, he
expected some bizarre proposal, which he

would probably have to ridicule if he were to keep his own feelings in order. But when she spoke, he did not feel as if there were anything bizarre in it ; there was earnest—desperate earnest—an earnest which in some subtle way communicated itself to him, and forced him to see and understand how hard was the fight with her, how passionately she struggled to do what should be both right and effectual for her purpose.

' Mr. Lawford, do you remember my telling you once that I trusted your face when I first saw you ?'

'Was I likely to forget the assurance from you ?' he rejoined, looking grave, but speaking a little sarcastically.

' You may laugh at it, but what I said I meant, and I think I cannot be quite wrong in my impression. I trust you still. Whenever in my own mind I think of some one to whom I could tell something, or whom I could ask to do something that other people would call difficult, I think of you.'

'You do me a great deal of honour,' was the reply.

Peril heeded not his words. He saw that her whole mind was concentrated on her errand.

'And it is because I feel so confident in you that I have asked you to come here, quite sure that you would not misunderstand my motive.'

'I hope I do not misunderstand it, but I can't say I understand——' he began, still somewhat carelessly.

She laid her hand upon his arm.

'Dear Mr. Lawford!' said she, with a grave sweetness which stabbed him, and made him curse his attempt at levity, though it had been used in self-defence, 'I beg you very much to listen to me. When you have heard me, I will submit to whatever you think proper to say. I shall be in your hands.

But now I am in great earnest, and great suspense.'

' I am at your service, Miss Nowell.'

' Then I must tell you, first—for I wish to be quite open with you—that I have had a grievous dispute with Mrs. Trelawney, though I am very fond of her. She has quarrelled with me because I hinted that I did not think she ought to tell me whom I should marry.'

' She will be cut up if you decline to marry Stephen Harkland,' said Lawford, looking her straight in the face.

' I have refused him. She is very angry. I hope it will be over some time. I am conscious that very few young women have to speak about—things—like this—in this way. It makes me unhappy, but I feel that I have to do it.'

She paused. Lawford said nothing. His heart was beating fast and ever faster; he could scarcely sit still in his place; and the reason for this was, he told himself, a most absurd one—the reason, namely, that Peril had 'sent that boy about his business.' Paul had had his own fears, hardly confessed even to himself, lest she should end her difficulties by the easy method of marrying Stephen Hark-land.

'Mrs. Trelawney wanted Mr. Harkland to have my money—the money which she wishes me to think is mine, and which it is the one object of my life to get rid of.'

'Yes.'

'So she is vexed for more reasons than one. For my part, I am tired of my false position; I am tired of being gaped at and shown about as the great heiress; I am tired of being alone in the world with no one who cares for me; I am tired of being a sham, and a delusion, and a snare to people—like Mr. Harkland, or anyone else. For all that they

tell me about my " position," and all that, I
am a very miserable and a very friendless
creature.   I am going to ask you a most
unheard-of thing—to get me out of my
difficulties.'

   ' I am afraid you overrate my powers,' he
said, while his heart seemed to leap to his
throat, and he felt a singing in his ears, a
surging in his head.   ' But if you will indicate
the way in which——'

   ' I *think*—I hope—it would not be an unpleasant thing to Katty, whom I love and
honour,' she began in a somewhat irrelevant
way ; and then suddenly, before he knew what
she was doing, she had slipped from the little
wall, and was kneeling in front of him with
her hands pressed upon his, as if she would
have tried to hold them down.   ' Don't think
me a bold, immodest girl,' she said in un-
varnished diction ; ' think of me as an unhappy woman, who, if you accede to her

prayer, will humbly try to serve you all her life—Mr. Lawford—Paul—will you marry me ?'

His first thought, words, action, were strange ones :

'Peril, do not kneel before me,' he whispered hastily ; 'rise up—sit here !'

With a strong pressure she held his hands down, continued still to kneel, and said again, but with the steadiness beginning to waver in her wild glance :

'Will you marry me, Paul ?'

It would be absurd to attempt any depiction of the thousand thoughts and arguments that flashed in a few seconds through Lawford's heart and brain. The for and against—the misery and the happiness that might come out of such a thing—all the host of prudential scruples—all the promptings of love and passion, coupled with the idea that this, which he wished for more than anything in

the world, had come to him unsought—he
had not had to go through the misery of
battling with all that the world would say
about fortune-hunters and heiresses—she here,
on her knees, asked him to do that which he
desired above everything else to do : both
these sides of the question flashed through his
mind. And lastly came the better feeling, the
purest feeling of them all—he loved her, not,
as she had once said that Nowell loved
Margaret Hankinson—as his saint on earth ;
there was not a thing that was saintly about
her—but very much indeed as the 'woman
he loved and wanted to marry.' She was
wretched and bewildered, and he could take
her out of her difficulties, and perhaps in time
she might come to care for him—that for the
consent : on the other hand, he was sordidly
poor ; he had poor relations, he wanted money
sorely—every tongue would cry out what a
grand thing he had done for himself, and

what a bad bargain she had made; and lastly, there was not that love on her side which could have made these considerations of less value than a pin's point in the scale. She would become his wife, not because she supremely wished to do so, but because to do so was more tolerable to her than to remain in her present position. Look at it either way, the benefit would really be the greatest to her, would seem the greatest to him. This debate has taken long to write; thought flashed it, and with fuller detail, in a few moments through his mind. While she was still looking up at him with strained, dilated eyes, face haggard with suspense, and lips bitten to keep herself from sobbing hysterically, he had made up his mind—to take the risk which was certain—the reward which was possible.

'Do not look so frightened!' he said, in the gentlest tone he could summon to his tongue.

'I understand it all—I know what prompts you; and I will marry you, Peril, when you choose.'

'Oh—h !' she sobbed ; and flinging her arm upon his knee, laid her head upon it and wept, while her whole form shook with sobs.

Something, whether instinct or reason, came to Paul's aid in the crisis, and stood him in good stead. He did not speak to her ; he did not attempt to quench her tears, or hush her sobs ; he took her disengaged hand, and held it in his, and was silent, till the storm which marked the reaction from her suspense, shame, and strained anxiety as to how he would receive her 'prayer,' as she very truly called it, was nearly over. And while they were thus silent, he began to realize more truly what had happened. There began to steal into his mind, with a sense of concreteness and reality, the idea that she—this girl whom he loved, and whom he had renounced utterly and entirely as being for a thousand reasons quite out of his reach—quite set apart from him, had of her own accord approached near to him—was going to be his wife. Despite all the strangeness, all the adverse side of it, that thought became nearer and nearer—more and more overwhelming. For though she had been driven by stress of circumstances to do this thing, to ask that which it is said to be a shame for a woman to ask ; though she might truly have chosen almost where she would ; though there was Stephen Harkland waiting for her, her dear friend Mrs. Trelawney ready to smooth out all obstacles, and make it easy for her to do, if done it must be ; though she might have gone about the business, or got some one else to go about it for her, in a thousand other ways—the fact remained that she had chosen this way—had sent for him, Paul Lawford, whose poverty she knew, whose faults and failings he had never tried to disguise from her, and had committed herself unreservedly into his hands.

He looked down at the beautiful, dusky head that was bowed upon his knee, as if the more effectually to hide her face from his gaze; he felt at last that she faintly pressed his hand with hers, as though to assure him that she understood his silence and his delicacy, and a passion of love and tenderness overtook him, and almost overwhelmed him. True, all was dark now; she was prostrate, ashamed, bewildered with what she had done, but it would all be well. And when the first dismay of her deed was over, and her courage had returned to her, then he would get his indemnification for the reserve and the reticence he was obliged to maintain now; for he literally dared not address to her any word of endearment, or offer any caress, or do anything except hold her hand as he was doing, and wait until she looked up or spoke.

*   *   *   *   *

'You must forgive me,' she said, before they parted, ' if I am stiff and stupid. I feel bewildered. I do not understand anything, except that I am going to be free, and to have a new life before me. Sometime later, I will try to show you that I can be better, gentler than I have been, if you will have patience with me. I know you are very patient.'

He felt a strong impulse to tell her that patience was a very much easier virtue to practise in some cases than in others, but held his peace, and she went on :

' Then you will tell no one, not even Katty, until you have arranged everything ? No one must know—of my friends or relations, I mean — because, if they knew, they would of course try to stop it ; and I do not mean to be stopped. When you have decided what we are to do, and how it is to be settled, then—we will tell Katty, won't we? because——'

'Don't distress yourself,' said he. 'I will arrange it all. You must give me a little time for consideration, and try to exercise that virtue which you admire so much, and possess so largely, and——'

'I know I am very impatient. I will try to be less so,' said Peril.

Paul was so enchanted with the sort of softness and change which had come over her, that he lost his head a little, and his sense, and reasoned to himself as if it—this docility and gentleness—were going to last for ever. Like her, he foresaw no backslidings. He let himself be deluded with the idea that patience would come in a day—nay, in an hour; that one short spell of violent emotion, one sudden deed of proportions which to him and to her appeared heroic, could change a nature. The elation of his joy was so great that he had even already begun to forget that what had raised him to such a height of happiness had been a desperate expedient for her. They were about to part, and as she made her promise of patience, Peril looked at him with pathos, and a soft dew in her dark eyes, and with lips that trembled a little. He answered this look with a prolonged gaze which caused her face to be troubled ; and raising her hand in both of his, pressed his lips upon her fingers, long and tenderly. He felt it more than he could compass to let her go without any sign that there was a bond between them, stronger than that of mere acquaintance.

'Good-night !' said she, in a very unsteady voice. 'I think you are very generous, and very, very good. I am grateful to you.'

She bowed her head, and went down the little path leading into a lane by which she

could get in at the farm-entrance of Stanesacre House. Lawford stood for a few
moments in the centre of the little spot which
had been the arena of their parley. It was
but a little corner, sheltered by a buttress of
the church wall, with two tumble-down old
tombstones, and the low stone wall on which
they had sat, with some tall, overgrown
yellow buttercups shooting up in one corner,
and a carpet of soft, sweet grass. An hour
ago, he had never stood in this spot before;
now, let him travel whithersoever he would,
it—this few feet of neglected ground, with its
glimpse of the chimneys of Stanesacre, its
distant view of a sort of arc of grey sea and
greyer sky—would stand out more distinctly,
more vividly, with a greater significance in
his mind, than any other spot on the face of
the earth. Where Peril had been kneeling at
his knee, the grass was crushed and levelled,
and certain small wild flowers had been

laid low—some little tufts of the blue milk-wort. He stooped and carefully gathered them, and bound them together with a little piece of grass. She had no need of a souvenir. Perhaps he had a dim idea that sometime, when years and life had bound her to his side, and showed her that she had not deceived herself in trusting herself to him, he could show her these little flowers, and tell her whence they came, and say to her, ' Do you remember ?'

CHAPTER III.

THE DAY THAT HAD NO END.

MR. WISTAR, one fine, hot May morning, slept the heavy, comfortable sleep of the substantial man, and dreamed, it may be, of wheat and cereals, or of sheep and the 'heavy beasts.' He snored away, and the time was towards six on a glorious morning. Mr. Wistar's room looked eastwards—towards the sea, but not upon it, because of the sheltered situation of the house behind hills and trees. But the brilliant morning sun streamed in through the spotless white linen blind and muslin curtains, also white as driven snow. Oh, the good

consciences, and above all the good diges-
tions, which allow the body to go on slumber-
ing on a bright summer morning, in these
country rooms, where the sun streams in
dazzling, through white curtains and blinds,
upon a white bed, and strikes clearly upon
white ceiling, white paint, and as often as not
walls papered with a 'neat' pattern, which is
likewise as nearly white as possible! Unknown to the inhabitants of such chambers
the horrors of insomnia, the need for shroud-
ing curtains and blinds that shall keep the
light out, instead of letting it in.

Mr. Wistar was very regular in all his
habits and customs, and in none more so than
in those which relate to the hours of going
to sleep and wakening up again. It was his
invariable rule to wake at six every morning
in summer, and at seven in winter. Summer,
with him, began on the 1st of April, and
ended on the 30th of September; and so

regular were his habits, so unalterable his convictions on the subject, that the transition
was usually made without the least difficulty.
' There's nothing like accustoming yourself to
a thing,' he would say. By this time, of course,
past mid-May, he had got well into the swing
of it ; and promptly on the stroke of six, Mr.
Wistar's eyes opened, and no dream, however
enchanting, could keep them shut after that
moment.

This morning, his dreams went off to the
subject which had greatly occupied his waking
thoughts of late—the great horse fair on
Askrigg Moor, which would come off in a
month or so, and to which he must of course
go. An exciting vision of a stampede amongst
the horses nearly woke him up. The heavy
thumping and thud of their hoofs over the
hollow turf became so loud and so importunate
that his eyes were fairly driven open ten
minutes before the usual time, and he slowly

began to realize that not horse-hoofs at all, but knuckles (probably human) on his bedroom door, kept up a perpetual drumming, and had in fact awakened him.

'Eh—what !' he called out vaguely.

'Uncle ! I never did know any man sleep in the way you do. It is quite disgraceful !' cried a clear, ringing voice.

Raising his head, with gaping mouth, his gaze encountered the head of his niece, clothed in a black poke bonnet and long feather, thrust in at his half-open door. At the sight of his extravagant, voiceless surprise, the head abruptly disappeared, and the sound of laughter, not loud but irrepressible, came from the outside.

'Now then, none of your marlocks, Peril ! What's the meaning of this ?'

She put her head in again, came into the room, and up to his bedside, and said, still laughing :

'How you forget things! I'm going to Darkingford—you know all about it. The dogcart is at the door, and I'm going to call for Mrs. Woodfall on my way. She will see me off, and return home to breakfast.'

'Oh, ay! I remember!' he said, pacified. 'Well, be off with you! For my part, I prefer travelling at a more suitable hour.'

'I prefer this. I shall reach Darkingford in time to get some business accomplished. I may be there two or three days. At any rate, I will write to you from there when I have seen Mr. Hankinson. Good-bye, dear!'

She put her hands round his old face and gave him a kiss, and a nod and a smile, and said :

'It has just struck six, and you are longing to get up.'

In a few moments more he heard the crunch of the wheels as the dogcart turned out of his garden and went up the lane. He got up, and went through the ceremony of dressing himself, in placid contentment and serenity. Some days ago, Peril had announced that Mr. Hankinson wanted to see her on business, and that she must make a pilgrimage to Darkingford ; and he had heard her discussing this very arrangement with Mrs. Woodfall—the going by the early train to York, instead of the late one, and thereby arriving at Darkingford by noon or soon after, instead of at eight in the evening. It was all right, and he hoped that Thomas, the man, would not linger on the way home, as he would want 'the cart' during the forenoon. So the honest old yeoman went contentedly about his day's work, and pictured his niece on her way to Darkingford. So she was in a way, but not by the direct route that he imagined.

The dogcart stopped at the gate of Wiswell Grange, and Katty was standing there waiting in bonnet and shawl. She

climbed in and shook Peril's hand, but said
not a word. Thomas, the driver, was there,
and no conversation was possible.

It was nearly a six-mile drive into Foulhaven ; they pulled up at the entrance of the
station in ample time for the 7.30 train, and
the two women got out, and left the man with
the trap outside. They were secure from his
observation, if they feared it ; for he drove off
to an inn a few hundred yards away, there to
water his horse and refresh his own inner
man until the whistle from the station should
warn him that it was time to return for Mrs.
Woodfall.

At that early hour there was scarce a soul
about. The day was not a market-day, and
except upon those occasions, the early morning
trains were little patronized at Foulhaven.
No one with whom they were acquainted was
on the platform at this time. One or two
farmers, both men and women ; an early

local mail, and some labourers—these were all the loiterers. Peril went to the booking-office, and asked for a first-class ticket to Yarland, which was a long way indeed from Darkingford. Then she and Katty stood by the carriage-door and said a few words to each other, but not many.

'It was good of you to come down with me,' said Peril. 'I should have turned coward at the last if you hadn't.'

'You have no need to turn coward,' said Katty, with a certain gentle reproof in her tones. 'Nervous you may be, I don't wonder; but you need not fear the man into whose hands you are giving yourself. I ought to know, and I say you need not.'

Peril made no answer. It was time to get into the train. She suddenly turned to Katty, and clasped both her hands.

'Oh, Katty! if I am doing wrong!'

'I am certain you are not,' replied the

other confidently. ' Give me a kiss, and give my love to Paul, if it occurs to you to remember such a thing ; and God bless you in what you are doing, and give you happiness !'

They kissed each other. It was a farewell kiss in more ways than one. In another moment Katty was alone on the platform.

Peril placed herself in the corner farthest away from the ' stopping side,' and looked out at the landscape through which the train slowly plodded, and wondered if she was doing right, and tried to understand what she *was* doing.

It was a fair and exquisite land through which the train carried her, travelling gradually northwards, and edging away from the coast. It stopped at every station, and the last part of the journey was diversified by constant views of a noble and beautiful river, which seemed to grow ever wider and wider, stronger and stronger. At last they glided

into a station belonging to a quaint, sleepy-
looking old town with red roofs, and the inevitable river. A large sign testified that
this was Yarland. Peril now went to the door
and looked out, scanning the faces of those
waiting on the platform. Some one flashes on
her sight, who stands watching with a somewhat eager expression, and, seeing her, comes
quickly up. Her heart gives a throb, but it
is not a throb of joy or delight.

Excitement, fear, suspense—above all, hesi-
tation and shrinking from the moment which
now seems so portentously and oppressively
near—all these pass through her mind, and
all are chased away by a last effort of determination as the door of the carriage is
opened, and her hand is clasped in that of
Paul Lawford.

' I thought the train was never coming,' he
said, as he handed her out.

' Is it late ? It seemed to me to fly along.

I felt sure it must be ever so much before
its time . . . if it had been—if you had not
been there——'

'What?' he asked.

'I should have gone on,' said Peril, in a
voice which sounded almost sullen.

The 'patience' which she had promised to
practise had been long a-coming. Lawford,
looking into her face, understood that there
was something of touch-and-go about the
whole business. But, he assured himself,
there was no drawing back for her now ; and
when once she was his wife, he still believed
in a sort of magic spell or talisman which this
consummation was to bring into play.

'Is that the church?' she asked, abruptly
pointing to where, hard by, a spire rose into
the air, on the bank of the river.

'No ; not that one. It is at Falconhill, about
half a mile off. I thought you would prefer
it, as it is still quieter than this. You see, the

Yarlanders have nothing to do but gossip.
Since Rivermouth arose nearer the sea, they
have had no trade here, so they spend their
time in studying the affairs of all the strangers
who pass through their town, and in abusing
the Rivermouthians to whoever they can get
to listen to them.'

' Oh, you must have found it rather dreadful living amongst them for three weeks.'

' It has not been too exciting. This way !
I hope it won't tire you to walk. To take a
fly here, is an episode which excites the
greatest attention, so——'

' I had much rather walk,' said Peril, as
they passed out of the village, and turned
along a beautiful leafy lane ; and she put up
her sunshade, and they strolled along, much
as if they were taking a country walk before
lunch.

After all, half a mile is covered in a short
time, even when one is strolling—a fearfully

short time it seemed to Peril ; and then they stood at the gate of a strange, dim church-yard, which was shady and quiet by reason of many large, broad-boughed old trees.

In less than half an hour they stood again in this same shady, dim churchyard, and heard the birds chirp, and saw the sunbeams come slantingly down through the tree-boughs. It was even yet not noon : nothing outside was changed, but what had been done was irrevocable. A few words quietly spoken, a ring put on her hand, had—though everything looked so much as it had done before—stripped her of the burden that she had found greater than she could bear ; and had, in-cidentally, given her, body and soul, with all the worldly goods she possessed, into the absolute power and control of this man at her side. It was of this, and nothing but this, that she could think just at the moment, in a paroxysm of suspense and apprehension.

After all, what did she know of Paul Lawford? and what security had she that he
would not even now break the bargain he had
made with her? which was—to let her go on
alone to Darkingford to-day, settle her
business there by telling Mr. Hankinson
what she had done, and desiring him to communicate with Nowell; and then he, Paul,
was to join her on the following day, and they
were to go—she did not know where—she
had left all that to him; and he might have
been honest about it, or he might not. It
was in his power to do as he chose about it.
The outcome of this doubt and suspicion was
the question asked, almost breathlessly :

'How soon can I get away again? When
will it be time for me to go on to Darkingford?'

'Much too soon for my wishes; but I dare
say not half soon enough for yours,' said
Paul. 'Not till four o'clock this afternoon.'

'Four o'clock! and it is not yet twelve!'
she exclaimed, in a voice which betokened
her dismay. 'Suppose anything were to
happen! Suppose anyone I knew saw me!'

'That is in the last degree improbable;
but even if they did, they would only see you
with your husband—there is nothing wrong
in that, that I know of!' he retorted; and she
felt that her words and her wild desire to
escape must have stung him. She hung her
head, but could not induce herself to say anything gentler. 'I have settled what to do,'
he continued. 'You must have got up at
some unearthly hour, and you look quite
exhausted now. You will come back with
me to the inn at Yarland, where I have been
staying, and have something to eat. Then I
propose rowing you up the river as far as
Prior's Dale, and letting you go from there
instead of here—the station you passed before
you got here, you know. It will pass the

time; and if I must tell the truth, Peril, it is a little more than I can stand, even to please you, to make myself so cheap as deliberately to see my bride off by a train and remain behind myself. If you have not a very great objection I shall go with you as far as York, and leave you there; you will, by that time, be on your way to Darkingford.'

Peril had not a word to say against these arrangements. Something in his tone convinced her that he was keeping good faith with her—was, in fact, treating her a great deal more generously than she was treating him. She could not cast off her dismay at what she had done; she felt like a frightened animal which has done wrong, and sees its master awaiting it, but with a chain in his hand, by which to fasten it for the future to one place in his own vicinity.

' I will do whatever you choose,' she said at last, with a vast and obvious effort. ' I am sure you are very kind to have arranged everything in the best way.'

'Everything that I choose,' said he, smiling a little sarcastically and wistfully at the same time. 'If I could believe that, Peril, I should speedily let you know that I choose something more gentle than what you are giving me now; but never mind—let us go on to the inn.'

Conscience-stricken, she walked in silence by his side, with ever the feeling of oppression at her heart, and the sense of coming evil and disaster growing stronger and stronger. Mechanically she partook of the meal he had ordered; and when Paul's land-lady—who, of course, knew all about it— begged to offer her her good wishes, she looked at her as if she did not understand her, and in a manner which roused the good woman's liveliest apprehensions with regard to Mr. Lawford's future happiness, for she had come to like him, and feel an affection for him—as everyone did except, it would seem, Peril.

'How long will it take to row to Prior's Dale?' asked Peril, again betraying her anxiety to be gone.

'Nearly two hours. Don't be alarmed; I will not make you late.'

＊　　　＊　　　＊　　　＊　　　＊

At last they had said good-bye to Yarland, pushing away from its sleepy shore, with the poplars growing along the river's bank, and were in mid-stream on a broad and much-curving river. It was high, blazing after-noon. Here was no evening hush or cool-ness. It seemed to Peril that from the time she had left the quiet, dewy garden and the hoary, shady orchard at Stanesacre, the sun had been growing hotter and hotter, and beating down with a more and more pitiless glare on to her head and into her heart, and

that this was the culmination of the intolerably
bright and obvious day. She felt less and
less like a real person—less and less able to
comprehend that she had really done something which had significance. All the feverish
day, which seemed to have been a hundred
hours long, must be some strange dream from
which she would awaken, perhaps to find
herself back in her convent at Rio, with no
more exciting episodes to look back upon, or
forward to, than her games with her play-
fellows, or an occasional visit to the house of
some of them in the holidays. If she might
only go back to the time before all this, how
good she would be, how meek, and docile,
and self-sacrificing!

'Peril!' said Lawford's voice, and she came
to herself with a start, and saw that he was
resting on his oars, and that they were in a
part of the river with sloping green meadows
on either side, with alders and rushes dipping

down to the water's edge, and here and there hedgerows white with hawthorn, dividing one field from another. At the end of the broad and solemn 'reach' of the river on which they paused, stood a noble cluster of fine trees, grave and still in the windless air. It was truly a very fair scene, such a scene as one of our English artists would paint *con amore*, and would show the broad lights and shadows flecking the hillsides, the opaline crystal of the river, the massive beauty of the trees, the peace of the whole scene, as no other can. They paused. The water rolled placidly onwards, escaping from under the keel of their boat towards Yarland and Rivermouth, and the big salt ocean north of Wiswell. 'I want to ask you something,' he said, when he saw that she looked at him.

'But do not let us be late for the train, or I shall be obliged to stop at Prior's Dale.'

'Is not that offering me a handsome

premium to *be* too late for the train ?' he said, a little bitterly. 'If you could manage to believe that I am not bent upon tricking and cheating you, Peril—why, so much the better. What I want to know is, shall I find you to-morrow at Mr. Hankinson's, or at Great North Street ?'

'I had never thought of it. I shall go to Mr. Hankinson's. They won't be ready for me at Great North Street. Miss Hankinson will take me in, especially when I have ex-plained my errand to her. Yes, you will find me there to-morrow afternoon.'

Lawford could not altogether repress the look that came over his face, expressive of his pleasure in this promise, his hope in what it implied. She saw this look, and a shade crossed her own face. Whether she were vexed or fearful, who should say ? She frowned, turned her face away from him, and leaning over the side of the boat, drew her hand through the rippling water. This continued for a little time, when she looked up again with the same expression of half-frightened, half-defiant suspicion in her face, a look which did not do much to reassure him as to the promise of happiness in their immediate future ; she looked at him thus, and then, whether out of bravado, or because she had quite lost her head and scarce knew what she was doing, drew her hand from the water, wiped it dry on her handkerchief, and with an almost stealthy look at him, proceeded before his eyes to pull the ring off her finger, which he had that morning put there. He saw the action, started, paused in his rowing, and half rose from his place. She looked at him hardly and coldly.

' It will be best,' she said ; ' I am afraid of anyone seeing it ; one never knows whom one may meet, and I have a fancy that no one shall know what has happened until I myself have told the people whom I wish to learn it first.'

She spoke drily and indifferently, pulled her purse out of her pocket, and began to search amongst its pockets for a safe receptacle for the ring.

'Peril!' he exclaimed in a deep voice of both pain and expostulation, so strong that she was arrested for a moment, and looked at him and said:

'Well?'

'Do not—I beg you, if you will take it off, not to put it into your purse amidst all your odd coins, which you might lose or mislay any minute. How hard you are! Do me the grace of hanging it round your neck, and hiding it—pray do!'

Her face flushed against her will, and balancing the ring rather awkwardly in her fingers, she said:

'But I—I really have nothing with me that

I could tie it to. When I get home, if you like—no, then I shall not need to conceal it. I think my purse is the safest place for the present.'

'Stop, you shall not say you had nothing to fasten it with,' said he hastily, as he let the oars go, and after a few moments unfastened something which had hung round his own neck, concealed by his shirt. It was a slender golden chain, to which hung something— Peril could not see what—but perceived a gleam like gold that shone. This something he quickly covered with his hand, unclasped the chain, placed the trinket, if trinket it were, in his breast-pocket, and handed the little chain across to her, looking at her all the time with an expression which she could not properly understand, though it agitated and troubled her.

'Take this; it will be the only thing I shall have ever given you,' he said. 'It has

never left me for many a year; do you take
and fasten your ring upon it.'

Impressed and overcome, she knew not
why, Peril silently took the chain, and
threaded the ring upon it, then paused a
moment, asking:

'What is the thing you had upon it?'

'Perhaps sometime I may tell you. At
present you would not care to know—if ever
you do, I will show it you,' he said; and his
tone was such that she became silent.

But as she placed the chain about her own
neck, which had hung for so many years round
his, and which was yet warm from its resting-
place, she felt a strange thrill and shiver
strike through her—a sense of depression, dim
and vague—a consciousness that perhaps that
path of renunciation, on which she had
believed herself fairly started, was as yet
closed to her—a glimmering idea that as a
matter of fact she had been exerting her will

strongly in opposition to circumstances, and instead of submitting or renouncing, had been very determinedly trying to carry all before her in her own way.

She pushed both chain and ring securely into concealment, and began to pull on her gloves again, while Lawford resumed his hold of the oars. And still, while they contrived to move over the short distance they had yet to traverse, the sun shone upon them —hot, high and unwinking—the river flowed broad and stately ; ever and anon some grand hanging wood, some fine old house, came slowly, as it were, floating into view, and floated out of it again ; ever and anon, turning her eyes away from this still and dreamy land, so forlorn and solitary, they encountered the figure of her companion, strong and graceful, whose practised strokes sent the boat swiftly cutting through the opposing current, and whose eyes, when they rested upon her, had

ever in them an expression which set her
heart beating, and made her almost hate him;
a lover's look, in fact, one of the factors on
whose significance she had placed all too
small a value in her calculation of the sum of
events.   Characteristically enough, she had,
in the excitement of the present day, nearly
forgotten what had brought it about.   By
the time they landed at Prior's Dale, she was
thinking far less of the deliverance from her
burden which she had accomplished, than she
was regretting her own inconceivable hasti-
ness and folly in rushing into a marriage with
this man whom she had never loved, and
who, now that she was irrevocably tied to
him, she actively disliked.   It was with ill-
concealed impatience and weariness that she
endured his company as far as York; it was
with a sense of the profoundest relief that she
at last felt the train glide out of the station,
and averted her eyes from the last glimpse of

his figure as he watched her off. To this relief succeeded a feeling of the deepest and darkest depression—the reaction in part of the long hours of suppressed excitement and irritation through which she had this day passed—but also largely due to a profound conviction on her part that she had that morning consummated the greatest folly, the most egregious piece of wilful wrongheadedness of all the many similar acts which had distinguished her short career.

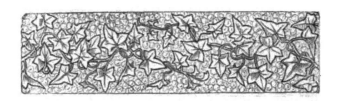

CHAPTER IV.

THE FIRST CONSEQUENCES.

NIGHT had covered the landscape, growing ever dimmer, smokier, and more unlovely as she approached nearer to Darkingford, the great centre of that vast, complicated network of towns and villages, mills and railways, which spreads over the greater part of Lancashire and creeps far into the West Riding of Yorkshire. Her excitement had all died away—nothing but the depression remained, and the unqualified shrinking from the lot which she had chosen for herself. She had gone so far as, in her own mind, to throw blame upon

Paul Lawford for having yielded to her prayer. It was so easy to remember that he ought to have withstood, now that she wished he had done so—so easy to forget how she had cast herself at his feet, presuming on a half-guessed knowledge of his love for her, and had besought him and pleaded with him in a way which must have caused ninety-nine men out of a hundred to have yielded. She forgot that; she knew that she would have given a very great deal to have her day's work undone.

With this sensation strong upon her, she alighted from the train at Darkingford, got into a cab, and directed the man to drive her to Mr. Hankinson's house in Queen Street. Half an hour's rattling over the noisy pavement, first through the flaring streets of the town, then along some quieter suburban ways, and here she was at her destination. She dismissed the man, took her little bag in

her hand, and rang. It seemed as if there
were long delay in answering her summons;
she had forgotten that it was close upon ten
o'clock—indeed, she had almost forgotten the
errand which took her where she now was.
At last the door was opened, and she asked
the maid if Miss Hankinson were at home.

'Yes,' said the young woman, in a rather
hesitating tone; 'did you want to see her?'

'Yes, I must see her to-night,' said Peril,
across whose mind it now began to dawn
that there doubtless was something odd in
the sudden appearance, at this hour, of
an unexpected guest—a young woman with
a weary face and a bag in her hand.

'Tell Miss Hankinson that I am sorry to
trouble her, but I must see her—Miss Nowell,
you must say. I will come in and wait till
she is ready.'

At the sound of her name, the servant
admitted her without more ado, but gave a

half-suspicious glance at her as she led her through the hall, and into Margaret's parlour. And indeed, Peril looked a little remarkable —deadly white and exhausted as she was with the excitement of the first part of the day, and the depression and long journey of the last. Her cheeks looked sunken, and her eyes hollow; and the garb of black which clothed her from head to foot threw out this paleness into strong relief, and added to her spectral appearance.

She seated herself, and the maid left her; and Peril waited, unconscious at first of the strange quietness there was over all the house, but presently beginning to realize it, and also the length of time that she was left sitting alone. The silence was indeed deep, and the deeper because it appeared to be every now and then broken by a sort of muffled whisper, or a soft, swift footstep. Once or twice overhead, Peril distinctly caught the sound of footsteps; but, taken all in all, the silence was profound and portentous, and it began to press upon her brain with a weight that she could hardly bear, and which made her feel hysterical. She felt as if she must scream, or laugh, or cry if it endured much longer. At length her straining ear was relieved by the sound of an actual footstep outside the door, which was opened directly afterwards, and Margaret Hankinson stood before her. Peril, though a moment before she had felt too utterly used up to experience a fresh sensation of any kind, started now at Margaret's changed appearance. She, too, had been suffering—and suffering, unless her appearance belied her feelings, from suspense, anxiety and fear. She was pale; she looked exhausted and harassed. There was a worn look on her mouth, and weariness and care in every line of her attitude.

That she also experienced surprise was evident. She stopped, on seeing Peril, with parted lips, from which came no sound; and thus the two young women confronted each other. It was Peril who spoke first, advancing a step or two.

'Miss Hankinson, you must not think that I am quite mad. I could not let you know of my coming, because—well, for various reasons. It was necessary that I should see Mr. Hankinson on very important business, and I——'

'That is impossible, I am sorry to say,' broke in Margaret's tones, in the measured cadences of a forced composure. 'My father is very ill—he was seized with paralysis at the office this morning; they brought him home, but he has never spoken since; he is living yet, but'—her voice continued quite steady, and yet it betrayed mental agony—'I can only hope and pray that, unless he recover his senses, he may be very speedily taken away.'

'Oh, how terrible!' ejaculated the other. 'How I grieve to have broken in upon such a trouble! I would have gone to Great North Street had I thought of telling them to prepare for me, but——'

'Do not distress yourself about that,' said Margaret, with the same steady composure. 'As soon as I heard you were here, I knew you would have come to stay. The maids are getting a room ready for you; and they will also get you something to eat if you want it. And in the meantime, you will pardon me if I go back to my father.'

'I never thought of his being ill,' said Peril in a low voice, as if she argued to herself on what had happened. 'Never—I wonder what I must do — to whom I must——'

'I can tell you nothing now,' said Margaret.

'I do not believe my father will live. In any case, I can only recommend you to take any business to the solicitors to-morrow. They would be able to——'

'My business concerns no solicitors,' said Peril, 'but you, and your father, and me, and Hugh Nowell.'

Margaret had been leaving the room, but she turned at this. 'My father—Hugh Nowell,' she remarked; 'pardon me, Miss Nowell——'

'I am not Miss Nowell any more,' said Peril, going up to her, and holding out her hand, to which she had restored her wedding-ring. 'Do you see this? I was married to Paul Lawford this morning, and Hugh—has got—his rights again.'

She was trembling violently. She held out her hands to Margaret imploringly, saying :

'Oh, do not tell me I have done wrong!

I have passed such hours of misery. If you condemn me, I shall wish I was dead.'

Margaret passed her hand over her forehead, and looked at her like one in a dream.

'I feel quite bewildered,' she said. 'Everything seems to come together. I was in great grief before this blow about my father, for——'

'Nothing has happened to Hugh?' almost gasped Peril. 'If you say anything has happened to Hugh——'

'Yesterday morning,' said Margaret slowly, 'I got a bundle of my letters to him, returned. One had been opened, but not by him. There was a note in the packet from a man called Laidlaw, with whom he had lodged. He went off up country with an exploring expedition, and nothing has been heard of them for many months. He left a few things behind, and a sum of money, and this man wanted to know what he was to do with it. That is all I can tell you.'

It was not like Margaret to speak thus, hardly, coldly, and categorically; but her faculties felt numbed with excessive grief and anxiety. She could call no life, no emotion, and no sympathy to her voice, but could just say off the words of her news as if she were reading out a list from a catalogue. Upon Peril, too, they seemed to fall without effect. She had sat down, and she stared at Margaret, still and motionless, and with a blank look of apathy in her eyes. She put up her hands, untied her bonnet-strings, and took it off her head, and said, in a voice of the greatest indifference—nay, with something like flippancy in her tone :

'It is just what I was born to—ill-luck on every side. I might as well have kept the money and my own freedom.'

'But,' said Margaret, struck, in spite of her

preoccupation with her own troubles, 'you say you were married this morning—are you alone ? Where is your husband ? I do not understand. Kept your freedom ! But if you cared for Mr. Lawford——'

'I never cared for him,' she said. 'I felt no dislike to him. He was indifferent to me then. I feel as if I loathed him now.'

Before Margaret could reply, the maid came to say that Miss Nowell's room was ready. She brought a tray in her hand, with refreshments on it. Margaret, to whom the whole scene was beginning to grow unbearably painful, and who wished to end it—for the present, at any rate—forced her guest to eat and drink something, and then, taking her by the hand, said :

'Come upstairs. You must go to bed. I can see you are almost fainting with weariness. You will sleep, and to-morrow things will look different—to both of us, I hope.'

Passively Peril allowed herself to be led to
the room she was to occupy. Mechanically
she returned Margaret's good-night, and found
herself alone.

She had bound herself, hand and foot.
She had with one fell stroke sacrificed everything—freedom, and fortune, and hope—that
right might be done ; and he for whom she
had done it had disappeared. Perhaps he
was dead, and would never know—nay, he
was dead ; or the star which ruled her destiny
had changed. Well, well ! Life was a sorry
coil for some people, and they were best who
were out of it. Out of it ! That recurred to
her mind, and she began to reflect that there
were ways and means of getting out of life—
either living or dead. You might kill yourself, but then you never knew what worse
you brought upon yourself, what malignant
shapes might be waiting upon the other side,
with all their implements of torture ready.

You might get out of it by carrying yourself
away, letting no one know whither you were
going, and remaining in seclusion for ever.
Again, the thought came over her mind of
those good nuns at Rio, and how peacefully
the time passed with them. To-morrow,
before Paul came, there might be time to do
a good deal : to get a long way from Darkingford and from him. She felt very tired ; she
would get into bed, and would think over the
best plan to pursue, for sleep felt far from her
eyes. So she undressed and laid her head
upon her pillow, and in five minutes was lost
in the profoundest sleep—a sleep which perhaps saved her from brain fever, or a complete
nervous break-down.

When she awoke in the morning, youth,
and strength, and perfect health had, in a
measure, triumphed over the terrors of the
day before ; but these latter had not left her
unscathed. She no longer felt the horrible

sensation as if a thick iron band were pressed around her forehead and head; but she felt weak and feeble in mind and body, almost too languid to rise, or move, or think. When she did get up she was surprised to find how her limbs trembled under her, how her heart beat at every slight sound, and the blood coursed with bewildering speed at every thought that came into her mind, just as it does with one who has been long ill with some consuming fever, and who begins to be healthy once more—but shattered.

Soon after she got downstairs she was joined by Margaret, who breakfasted with her. Her father was still in the same state, no change being visible for better or worse. During the vigil that she had kept by his side in the night, Margaret had had time to get her own thoughts and impressions into order; and then, and only then, had the full nature and importance of what Peril had done made

itself manifest to her. She had been too bewildered and too full of her own griefs and
fears last night to realize it. But now she
comprehended; and an awe, somewhat akin
to Peril's own, of the utter irrevocableness of
what she had done, took possession of her
mind. She, the woman of eight-and-twenty,
large - brained and large - hearted, felt her
widest sympathies overflow towards this wild,
impulsive, selfish yet generous creature, who
had done so mad and wrong a thing, with so
very good an aim, so true a purpose. With
her own powerful convictions on the subject
of unions of selfishness or convenience,
marriages made for money or policy, she
entered to the full into the feelings of terror
and regret which now possessed Peril's soul.
Such a child she seemed to Margaret, from
her eight years' vantage-ground; such a child,
and in many ways such a childish child. Un-
trained, untaught, undefended, she had battled

with her difficulties ; had seized upon what seemed to her a way of escape, and found herself in a labyrinth ten times more complicated. And this in order that Hugh Nowell, who, as his betrothed could not help feeling in her secret heart, had not showed himself perfectly unselfish in the matter, might not be defrauded of what she felt belonged to him of right. She was warmer and more genial to Peril this morning ; she talked to her, allowing the nurse to watch by her father. And she heard from Peril the reasons for her step ; heard of the letter she had written to Nowell, and of his reply to it—a revelation which shocked Margaret disagreeably.

‘ After that,’ said Peril, ‘ it became a matter of honour with me not to be beaten by him. It was a long time before I thought of this. It came into my head suddenly one night when Mrs. Woodfall had been telling me how poor they were, and how·they would have to

sell Wiswell Grange, and go to South Africa.
I felt as if I should not have a friend left.
And then, little Humphrey, whom I love,
came and put his arms round my neck and
kissed me, and showed that he was fond of
me. And then Paul, I saw how they
worshipped him who knew him best ; and I
said to myself I was safe with him, and that
if he would marry me I could not be very
miserable, unless I were really a very bad
young woman. So I asked him, and——'

'But, my dear, what were his motives ?'
asked Margaret anxiously ; and feeling, as
everyone did with Peril when the ice of her
first hauteur had been broken, a curious fascination and attraction to the moody, wayward creature.

'He has a very good heart,' said Peril.
'And I think—he cared for me. I never
would let him say so, but Katty told me.
She said I was too rich for him ever to have

asked me; but he was *very* glad when I asked him; and I do not see why everyone else should get what they want, and I should have *nothing*,' concluded Peril passionately.

'I think,' said Margaret gently, 'that, as Mr. Lawford cares for you so much, you had better go through with what you have done. I liked his face, though I saw so little of him. If you trust him, you will perhaps find that it is not only he who has got what he wants.'

Peril's face hardened, and Margaret, though she did not say so, had an inner conviction that if Lawford once succeeded in getting a grip of the girl's spirit, once managed to subdue her into agreement with him—mastered her, in short, at once firmly and gently, the crisis would be over, and Peril's storms and troubles practically at an end. Her secret doubt was whether the young man with the handsome, languid face and lazy blue eyes, whom she had liked for his pleasant look and graceful manner, and then dismissed from her mind, had the nerve, and the tact, and the strength, and the backbone, to render him capable of the task. For her part, she thought, if she had been a man, she would rather have encountered the most stormy sea, without help, than have plunged into matrimony with Peril Nowell.

CHAPTER V.

FREEDOM.

IT was still early, and still daylight, when the train that carried Peril southwards rolled out of York Station. Lawford, after watching it till he could see it no more, went into the town to an inn that he knew of, where he bespoke a room for the night, and then went forth again and strolled about, first in some gardens, and then, when they were closed, along a walk on the river-bank. Whatever might be going on in Peril's mind, what had happened was all the world to him, and he felt a boyish happiness and lightness of heart as he paced

about, and thought of all the incidents of that
long, dreamful day. Let come what might,
he thought, she was his wife; and nothing
could part them. He foresaw difficulties—
yes, he supposed there would be difficulties
in dealing with her; but he felt strong enough
to encounter them all, and overcome them
all. Chance—or Providence—some kind and
bountiful Dispensation, had given him the
one chance which would make it possible for
him to succeed with her; nothing short of
what he had now—the actual fact that he was
her husband—would have given him this, for,
so long as their relative positions had remained in their original condition—so long
as she had been the great heiress and he the
poor man at her gates, they would never
have approached one inch nearer to each
other, because he would never have made an
advance. Circumstances had so combined
together as to cause the advance to come

from her, without any shame either to her or to him ; and that being so, he felt confident in the future—felt the game in his own hands. He was full of compunction for her, and an unbounded tenderness. Her perversity to-day he attributed to the strange and bizarre position in which she found herself. It was natural enough in a girl of twenty to feel shame and embarrassment under such circumstances, and in a girl of her nature to put on hardness, and behave irritatingly in order to conceal what she felt. Endless patience alone would overcome those feelings on her part, and endless patience she should receive from him. He was sure that he could overcome her, because he was sure that he knew the worst of her; and she had done nothing yet which he did not feel strong enough to match and conquer on his own part.

Full of feelings like this, he slept that night

—yet more hopeful and buoyant he rose in the morning. The hours which he had to kill seemed long and wearisome ; he strolled about the city, and for a long time he sat in the great, cool minster, and listened to the organ-notes, and felt a good deal lifted up and exalted. He prepared himself then, all unconsciously, to do battle ; but the battle he anticipated consisted of girlish fears, spasms of suspicious pride, reluctance to submit to the yoke. Any such thing as prosaic, sordid matter-of-factness—anything mean, or anything repulsive, never occurred to him as possible. He arranged, as we all do, for what he expected. He had no weapon in all his armoury with which to meet the unexpected, though he knew, as well as most men, that the unexpected it is which usually happens. He would have admitted it readily —had it not been so, he would not have been Peril's husband now. It is this elaborate

provision for the expected with which our
thoughts are occupied—this naked helplessness in regard to the unexpected which
characterizes most of us, that causes the
imperfect, haphazard nature of some of our
most important actions; for, as the supreme
moments of our lives come almost always at
a time and in a manner the most unlike anything we have anticipated, generally bursting
upon us when the sky seemed clear, and no
great event in the least probable, so, it is
equally true, we meet these crises, not in the
best way, but as we can; as it occurs to us
at the moment when our nerves are all ajar,
our whole being in a state of startled excitement. Surely this is one of the things which
help to make noble conduct at great moments
so difficult—it is the consciousness we all
have of this which makes the most of us so
keenly appreciate anything like nobility or
presence of mind in a crisis; we are vividly

aware what a chance business it is, what a touch-and-go sort of thing, with sublimity on one side of a hair's breadth—bathos and pitiable inadequacy on the other.

Paul was no genius; nothing very brilliant or very bad, and no exception to the rule of chance just spoken of. When it was time he set off for Darkingford, and after travelling for what seemed to him a very long time, he arrived there, and made as speedy a way as possible to Mr. Hankinson's, his heart aglow with hope and love—full of a great longing to see her beautiful, perverse face, and take her into his own possession, and make her happy with him, as he meant to be happy with her.

Margaret's sitting-room again, full of the afternoon sun, and with stillness over all the house. And here he was left waiting for awhile till the door slowly opened, and Peril came into the room, closing it after her. She had a small bundle of papers, and a cheque-book in her hand.

'You have been engaged in business already, my—Peril?' he said, going quickly up to her; and as her hands were full of things, and she could not give them to him, he took the first attempt at an unfair advantage of her, put his arm around her waist, and kissed her cheek. It was cold, and she made no response. He saw a singular quietness and stillness in her manner. She had offered him no word of greeting, and now, when he paused and looked at her, she said, laying her papers down on the table :

'You haven't heard of the misfortune here, of course.'

'Misfortune—no; nothing that affects you, I hope?' he said quickly.

'Me, no!' she replied with contempt, and in a tone that stung him. She went on—'I am safe enough, and my money too. It clings to me like a burr that sticks to one's clothes, or pitch to one's fingers.'

'Please tell me what has happened, for it seems to have disturbed you.'

'In the first place, poor Mr. Hankinson is very ill. He has had a paralytic attack, and is dying, they think.'

'Dear me, I am very sorry. You will be anxious to get away.'

She gave him a look of such tragic import that he was half-vexed, half-inclined to laugh. He compromised, and smiled, and she answered the smile by saying in hard, incisive tones :

'The next thing perhaps you will be gratified to hear is, that Hugh has disappeared on some exploring expedition. He has not been heard of for months, nor the expedition, and Miss Hankinson's letters to him have been returned. Most likely he is dead, and this horrible money mine *yet !*'

'My poor child, don't break your heart yet. It does not at all follow that he is dead. He need not be. Most likely he is *not* dead.'

'I know better!' she said, with determination. 'I might have known how this would end! I knew yesterday morning, as soon as I walked out of that wretched church—I knew that I had signed and sealed my own doom, and that something dreadful was going to happen. It pressed upon my heart and my mind like lead, and grew heavier and heavier all the way here. *This* was the news that met me, and then I knew what it all meant. I feel as if there was a curse upon me!'

'That is morbid,' said he gently. 'Come away with me, and I will try and show you another side of the question. I think, I must say, that Hugh has shown great folly, not to call it anything worse, in joining such an expedition. If he had been a free man it would have been different; but when he had left Miss Hankinson behind him——'

'We won't discuss that,' said Peril sharply and hardly. 'I don't suppose we shall ever agree about it. You say he has behaved badly; I say he has been driven on to his end by my deed. I am sick of my life, and sick of the light of the sun, and of everything in this hideous, selfish world.'

'I will take you as far away from the world as you choose,' he said. 'And we will plan together how to ascertain what has become of Hugh, and restore him his money.'

'Ah!' she said, in the same dry, bitter way, 'I might have thought that very pretty once, but I am past it all now. I must give my life to something different from love-making in the country. I want to tell you something, and to ask you something,' she added,' as she drew a chair to the table, and sat down at it. 'Let me say out my say—

don't interrupt me, and I will try to make clear to you what I have been thinking of ; and I hope you will agree with me.'

Paul stood on the hearthrug with his shoulders against the mantelpiece, his hands clasped behind him, and he looked gravely down at her.

' Say on,' he said. ' I think you will come to my mind at last.'

' To-day—this morning—I have been into town and seen Mr. Redmayne, the solicitor. I told him what I had done. He held up his hands, but I think he was relieved : he is of the opinion that large properties should descend in the male line. But when I told him of this news which has come about Hugh Nowell, he became grave. He said it made it complicated. He says, too, that if Mr. Hankinson dies, and, as is probable, leaves his daughter his sole executrix, the administration of all this thing will be in her hands.

That is odd, isn't it? Would it not have driven Grandpapa Nowell wild to think of such a thing? It is enough to make him turn in his grave as it is.'

She paused a little, and then went on in a slightly husky voice, and her lips too, he noticed, looked dry and parched; but none of this gave him one merciful gleam of light as to what she was going to say to him, and he listened a little impatiently until it should be his turn to try and persuade her.

'I inquired what I was entitled to,' she said. 'He told me that for a good many years to come I should be entitled to exactly what would have been mine if Hugh had been here on the spot to claim his own. The law is slow about considering a man dead, or disposing of his property. That is, I, having broken the conditions under which I became mistress of the whole estate, continued to be entitled to the fifty thousand pounds which he left me, and, as a minor for one year more, to the income set apart for me till I came of age, eight hundred a year. Do you understand ?'

' Perfectly; but I don't see what——'

'Wait a moment; you will see presently, because you will have an important voice in it all. I have lived for a year with my Uncle Wistar, and they have regularly sent me the money for my maintenance. But one doesn't spend very much at Wiswell; and when I was abroad I spent my money like the Trelawneys, economically. I have got nearly five hundred pounds of my last year's income left. I do not want anything; a hundred pounds will last me for a year, and that makes twelve hundred, or nearly twelve hundred, to be correct; and after that, when I am of age, I shall have two thousand five hundred a year. If I 'were to keep the five hundred,

54—2

that would leave two thousand. Do you see ?'

'I follow your calculations perfectly ; but you must let me say that, just now at any rate, I would like to talk of something else. I am thinking of you, not your money.'

'I must talk of that, and of what it leads to. Paul '—with a sudden gesture she planted her arms firmly on the table, and looked into his face with eyes that had grown hard, or desperate, but which carried in them the spirit of determination—' I did wrong to marry you. I had no right to shirk my difficulties in any such way. If marriage had come in the ordinary way—if I had loved, and been loved, and had agreed to give up the money and take the man who was everything to me, I should have been right enough, it seems to me. But as it is, I was wrong.'

'Let us hope you will come to think differently. If——'

‘ I asked you to hear me out. I know I am in your hands. I know what the law is ; it gives a man absolute power over the woman who has married him. If he bids her, she must go with him and do what he likes, whether she likes or not. You can do that with me, if you choose. My life has been wretched enough ; you can make it a hell on earth if it pleases you. But I don't think you will, if I tell you that the idea of carrying out our bargain makes me feel—as if I should die in performing it. I know I have wronged you. I know I owe you some compensation ; and I wish to make all that lies in my power. This money that I have been speaking of, I want none of it. It is a curse to me, and a misery. I want to keep as little as I can—I will be very poor, and try to learn submission to my fate—but I know that you can use it as it ought to be used. It will free you from all your difficulties; you will never need to trouble about Humphrey again; it would give me a little happiness to know that this horrible money was being spent on anything so sweet and good. If you will take it and do what you like with it, and let me go away somewhere where I can hide and be forgotten—that is what I mean, Paul—if you will do that, oh, how welcome you would be to every penny I have, ten times told !'

As he did not at first speak, she went on hurriedly, while she pushed towards him the books she had had in her hands, as if to heap one persuasive argument upon another.

'I called at the bank and got this cheque-book, and gave them my new name, and said I supposed your cheques were the same as mine. They said, quite. That is the pass-book, and——'

She started and shrank together suddenly.

Paul burst into a loud, discordant laugh, harsh and dry, and without one note of amusement in it.

'Splendid!' he exclaimed, and put his hand to his head, as if to support himself under the excessive wit of the joke. 'Splendid! The master-stroke of all! Ha, ha! Oh, how rich! When Katty hears, how she will congratulate herself and me!'

He stopped abruptly. Laugh and words, harsh and dissonant as they were, had both stopped. He raised himself from his attitude of stooping backwards, and gave himself a kind of shake together; then made a step towards her, and stood close over her. His face was white to the very lips, and though he strove to speak, it was some time before any words would come. She, meanwhile, beginning to perceive that the emotions she had roused by her proposal were other than what she had calculated upon, was gazing up at him with wonder, in which some alarm was mingled.

'Peril,' at last he said, in a harsh, broken voice, which did not sound in the least like his own, 'if a man had come to me and proposed anything to me which implied such an opinion of me as is implied by what *you* suggest, I should have struck him across the mouth to choke him with his own insolence. As you are a woman, and, before the sight of God in heaven, the woman who is my wife, I can do nothing. I see now what you think about *me*—would that you had left me any delusion about yourself! I was a cur, it seems, who would swallow any garbage so long as he was paid to do it. It pains me, since I can imagine how disappointed you will be, to have to tell you that I am a man, the sort of man they call a gentleman, not the thing you think. Put your money away.'

She sat, almost cowering, gazing up at him like one paralyzed, and made no answer and no movement.

'I understand what you want,' he went on, and his tones had become more composed, but his words stung her, and she felt as if she burnt under them ; 'I understand what you want—or rather what you do not want. Peril,' his voice shook strongly for a moment, 'why, in heaven's name, do you suppose I married you ?'

She shook her head speechlessly.

'For your money? Because I was poor and pinched, and you could give me ease and plenty? When did I ever give you to suppose that ease and plenty were more to me than honour and honesty? There are men who do it, you think, ay, and women too, and I would not be too hard on them ; but I had set *you* up on a different pedestal. If anyone had told me you could give yourself

to a man who would sell himself to you for
your money, I would have told him he lied.
We are by way of telling home-truths this
afternoon. Let me explain myself clearly.
You have fallen so low, so unutterably beneath what I imagined it was possible for
you to sink to—for you have first married
me, and then showed me what you thought
me, and, in consequence, what creature you
could marry—so low you have sunk that I do
not think I shall ever care to look upon your
face again. Keep your money. Take your
freedom. I have lost all wish to deprive you
of it. You took me for a hound, and you
have married the hound and taken his name.
God forbid that I should ever meddle with a
woman who could do such a thing !'

Lawford picked up his hat, turned on his
heel, and walked out of the room and out of
the house.

An hour afterwards Peril was still in the

attitude in which he had left her—her arms spread upon the table, her head prone upon them, uttering every now and then a fluttering, low and broken crying, as of some animal which is mortally hurt.

CHAPTER VI.

AFTERWARDS.

ERIL might very likely have remained where, and as she was, for
hours, if nothing had disturbed
her—prostrate in mind and body, feeling as
if her life and any shred or ray of self-respect
which she might ever have possessed had
been stripped from her for ever. She felt
herself vile and an outcast. Paul's biting
words had opened her eyes in a way she had
never experienced before ; while she shrank
and writhed under the recollection of them,
she told herself after all that they were not
half strong enough to describe the truth.

She was all that he had said, and worse.
She had never taken him for what he said
she had; but she had felt careless about him,
had played with him in a violent and insolent
manner, and had finally offered him a gra-
tuitous insult, whose nature and extent she
understood the instant that he had ceased
speaking to her. He had doubtless spoken
the truth, and said no more than she deserved, when he had told her that she had
sunk beneath his contempt, and that she was
welcome to her freedom, for he had lost all
desire to deprive her of it. Now she understood what she had lost, and worshipped it in
proportion to its entire removal from her
grasp, or from the possibility of her ever
being able to approach any nearer to it.

. Round and round a circle of thoughts like
this her wearied brain went wandering, and
her body was every now and then shaken
with a little shudder as she recollected how

terrible Paul had looked, standing over her
with his changed face, his white lips, his
kind blue eyes turned cold as steel ; the
scorn, the unutterable, withering contempt
of his tones and gestures. If she lived to
be a hundred she could never outlive this
day, nor its shame, nor the fact that she had
shown herself so dense and so mistaken as to
commit this action. It branded her, in her
own mind, as effectually as if the tale had
been written upon her forehead for all to
read.

She heard no sounds in the house, no
movement, no entrance of anyone into the
room. The first thing that roused her was
the touch of a pair of hands on her shoulders,
and a woman's voice speaking her name—a
voice which was broken and thick with tears.
She raised her haggard face and saw Margaret, and, absorbed though she was in her
shame and her woe, she realized that there

was a change in the face of the other. She
had carried the fear of calamity in her expression before; now she wore the look
which tells that the calamity has entered and
been consummated, that the stroke has been
dealt.

'I did not know you were here,' said
Margaret. 'Has your husband not been?'

'He has been, and gone; and has told me
he never wishes to look upon my face again,'
said Peril.

'But, my dear child, you must not give
way to such fancies,' said Margaret sooth-
ingly, forgetting her own catastrophe.

'Don't touch me,' said Peril; 'you don't
know what a wretch I am! You don't know
what sort of a creature you are harbouring in
your house. I have only found out myself
this afternoon.'

The natural thought that came into Margaret's mind was one of pity for Peril. She

feared that Lawford had been specious and bad; she noted the cheque-book and the bank pass-book which lay upon the table, and she was filled with an uneasy apprehension; she seemed to see troubles looming up in a long vista for the unhappy girl who had married an adventurer, and had already begun to experience his ill-usage.

'Let us not talk about me,' said Peril. 'Something has happened to you, I can see. Is it——'

'It is all over!' said Margaret, in a broken whisper. 'He died with his poor tongue paralyzed, and his eyes trying to tell me something. Oh, my father! my father!'

Her grief allowed of tears. She bowed her head upon her hands, and rocked herself in her sorrow, and wept; and Peril watched her, and, for the first time in her life, felt the power and the necessity of offering consolation to another. Out of her own great misfortune she could make a comfort, by showing some one else how much worse her case was than that other's. She went and knelt down before Margaret, and said to her :

' Margaret, I know you are very sad, but I wish I was as sad as you are. I wish I had nothing worse to think of than you have, and that I could sit down and think how good my father had been to me, and how I loved him. Will you let me stay here for a little while ? I will give you no trouble. Will you let me explain now what has happened to me ?'

Margaret stayed her tears and listened while Peril told her what had taken place between her and Lawford. She reproduced each word of each of them throughout the interview—repeated them steadily, clearly, and distinctly—and wound up :

' I do not know what will become of me in the future. I think he will go back to Wis-

well, and to his sister, and will tell her what
I have done; and she will hate me, as I deserve to be hated.   I cannot go there.   Will
you let me stay with you?   I feel safe with
you; I feel as if I should not go quite mad
while I am near you.'

Margaret, ' large-brained woman ' as she
was, understood and sympathized with a
broad and great sympathy.   She knew in a
moment that, grief or no grief on her part,
here was a task ready to her hand, a need
and a want and a misfortune quite as great
as any she had ever battled with or tried to
alleviate in courts and alleys and slums of
the city.   It was here, under her own roof,
appealing to her for help, crying out for support.   She had always asked in her prayers
for the work that was meet for her; and if
the work came, it was surely her part to do
it, and not be fastidious as to the hour in
which it was given her to do.   Nay, she was

able to recognise the great truth that this task, by whomsoever set, whether intended or not, was qualified to alleviate her own sorrow, and to enlarge her sympathies. She realized this dimly; its influence was with her. Perhaps she actually put it in the more prosaic shape of saying that, since circumstances had thrown Peril on her protection, it would be inhuman not to afford it to her. In any case, she at once yielded full and hearty consent to the girl's prayer that she might stay with her. She told her to stay, and have no thought of going away—sorrow medicines sorrow. And in this house of mourning, Peril, in the stress of the shipwreck herself had made, or seemed to have made, of her life, found shelter and harbour, rest and an abiding-place, if not calm weather or cloudless skies.

*   *   *   *   *

And the days passed on and grew into

weeks, and she was still there, and remained there; and Margaret, in the solitude which had fallen upon her life, and in the work which had suddenly overtaken her, found consolation in Peril's company. The probation period in some lives comes late. Margaret Hankinson was eight-and-twenty, and hers had just begun.

As had been anticipated, her father's will left her his entire property, and constituted her its sole executrix and the administratrix of his estate. And, since Mr. Nowell's will had left his estate in Hankinson's management, it followed that during the suspense about Hugh, Margaret became practically the head of the great business as well as the executrix of her father's property. She had her task set, and it was an onerous one; but, as has been said, she was something of a genius. Her father's one false step, the divergence into speculations with his master's

money, he had long since made good. Mr.
Nowell's death, and the immense responsi-
bilities which had with it devolved upon him,
had sobered him, fortunately, instead of em-
boldening him, and had checked his tendency
to speculation. For the past year the business had been conducted on purely legitimate
principles. It may be added that, from the
time of Mr. Nowell's death, Mr. Hankinson
had been subjected to a kind of surveillance
which he had not experienced before, that
of the solicitors who acted in all legal concerns, and who of course now stepped in in
many things where formerly nothing would
have been needed but to get Mr. Nowell's
signature. Where they interfered, they investigated, and Mr. Hankinson had found it
best to keep within bounds. But they had
no power to buy and sell, or to manage any
commercial transactions. This now fell
entirely upon Margaret, and she proceeded

in a characteristic way. She had heard her father speak with approval of a certain Robert Marsden, one of the foremen, as being a man who had worked his way from the position of an office-boy—a lad who swept and dusted, and carried home six shillings a week to his mother—to his present place. Margaret went down to the office, sent for Mr. Marsden, and conversed with him, using her own judgment as to his capacities, and deciding greatly by what he said of his subordinates and fellow-officials. Her impression was a favourable one. She promoted Marsden to the post of head manager, subject to herself. She frankly told him of her ignorance, and that she would have to depend upon his honour and honesty; she exacted from him that no transactions should be accomplished without being first submitted to her, and added, that for the future her time would be devoted first

and foremost to this task. She approved of
the young man's quiet, homely, but shrewd
way of speaking, and was pleased to find
that he did not seem particularly elated by
his sudden promotion. She arranged with
him to be at the office at certain hours every
day, and, feeling that she could do no more,
went home again, full of anxiety, and with
her mind preoccupied with this new, strange,
and bewildering thing, which must henceforth
take up so much of her time and thoughts.
She set herself steadily to work to learn her
business, for it was literally that which she
had to do, with the additional anxiety of feeling that even while she was learning, as a
tyro, she was as much responsible as if she
had been a hoary-headed man of business.
She found she had been fortunate in her
choice of an assistant, partly, no doubt, by
chance, partly from her own pretty keen in-
sight into worth and character. But she felt

harassed and worn with the new and onerous
undertaking : it was not what she would have
chosen, it was not what she liked ; but it was
what she felt bound to do, and she did it,
though she felt her youth and her brightness
slipping away from her with wonderful
rapidity.

So was carried on a sort of romance of
commercial life, for it was nothing else—a
romance which caused emotions vivid enough
in those concerned in it, but was unknown
beyond their immediate circle. So it came
to pass that the vast estate of old James
Nowell passed virtually into the fragile
hands of 'a couple of lasses,' as he would himself have said ; and he had always felt and
expressed coarsely enough the most unbounded contempt for women in any matters
of business.

This digression is by no means intended as
a vindication of the capacities of women to

manage not only such little business as they may in the ordinary course of events be blessed—or cursed—with, but also such great businesses as this in question. Anyone who knows anything about our manufacturing districts does not need to be told that they contain business women, women who conduct their factories, buy their yarn and their weft, attend the markets, and compete successfully enough with their rough rivals—and they are rough indeed, sometimes. Nor would it be a new thing to some people to hear of women who, whether their names figure as members of the London Stock Exchange or not, are virtually members of that august confraternity.

Margaret Hankinson had no ambition to be a cotton manufacturer on a large scale, but circumstances forced the position upon her; and she accepted it, and along with it the other anxieties of those circumstances.

Not the least was the one attending the possible fate of Hugh Nowell. In the multitude of her concerns for his benefit if he lived—for that of his heiress, Peril, if he proved to be dead, Margaret had had literally no time for the indulgence of sentimental sorrows. Many a time, in the midst of her dry affairs, a sudden thrill shot through her as she felt a grim doubt about the use of them in any case. Hugh, for whose sake they were being made, might be dead; his bones might be bleaching now, in some lone recess of that mysterious land to which he had gone. She looked forward with sickening qualms to the prospect of long years spent in suspense : at the end of that time, whether he were living or dead, the law would treat him as if he were dead. The light of her life would have been quenched long before then, and—but then came a revulsion of feeling, a thankfulness for this work that had to be done, this drudgery that must be daily gone through at the risk of loss and disaster. It at least kept her thoughts from dwelling too intensely and too monotonously upon all the possible horrors that might have befallen the wilful, handsome, bright-faced lad who had taken her heart by storm, and overcome her better judgment, and been selfish with the airy, reckless selfishness of youth, which can sin so gracefully in this respect as to make us almost offer our congratulations upon the faculty it possesses of doing what it likes, without regard to others.

Margaret kept her own counsel. She was one day asked by Peril, who seemed to have sobered down into a very sedate, grave young woman, with wistful eyes and a melancholy mouth, 'if there were no means of making inquiries about Hugh ?'

Margaret almost smiled.

The question showed so very plainly how entirely he had passed, as an object of sentiment, out of Peril's heart, and, as it were, range of vision altogether. There was indeed no danger of any rivalry between them.

'Do you suppose I have not seen to that?' said Margaret. 'I have engaged a person, a man whom I know and thoroughly confide in, to go to Melbourne and make every possible inquiry. If human means can find him, living or dead'—and her brave mouth trembled for a moment, and her steadfast eyes filled—'I shall hear of him sometime. Did you really think I was sitting here quietly without making any attempt of the sort?'

Peril looked a little embarrassed; she felt a little shame to think how utterly indifferent she had become on this subject. Was it really possible or conceivable that love for Hugh Nowell, disappointment and anger at his slighting her, had been the original cause which had brought about her present position? Why, now, if it were not for Margaret's sake—for she adored her—she would have found it difficult to get up any keen hopes or fears about him. If she heard that he was dead, she would be sorry of course : it would be sad to think of a bright young life quenched so soon and so sorrowfully; but he would have brought it a good deal upon himself, as she had done, and it was better to die than live under such circumstances. As for thinking of him as an object of love or hate, as potent to cause a thrill of joy or fear in her, she felt half amused, wholly ashamed, as she conned over the past, and acknowledged that, incredible though it seemed, it had once been so.

There was another name, not that of Hugh Nowell, which she sometimes whispered to herself when she was alone, though she never spoke it aloud; and this name, and the image of him who bore it, had power to shake her to her very soul.

Margaret, when she had first heard of Peril's marriage, had thought vaguely to herself that if Lawford could master her, all would be well. He had mastered her, so that in every thought and every action she referred to him mentally ; he had subdued her, mind and soul—not of set purpose, but by chance. He had mastered her in such a way that, though she never spoke his name, her whole life was a sort of dedication to him ; now that she had the prospect of never seeing him again, he filled a greater space in her thoughts, her ideas, her prayers—when she made them-—than any one of the real and present things and persons she encountered. Every new face, every fresh conversation, every book she read, picture she saw, or strain of music that she might hear, she interpreted, not of her own natural mind, but by some ideal measure, suppcsed to belong to him. She had wronged and insulted him. She had treated him like a cur— so he had told her. He had on the spot, and with the speed of lightning, showed her that he was a man, and one who was stronger than she was; and she had been his slave from that moment.

It seemed a pity, if he wished for compensation—of which, however, he gave no sign— that there appeared to be no chance of his ever learning this fact.

PART IV.

THE LIFTED BURDEN.

CHAPTER I.

THE BEGINNING OF THE END.

IT was November, eighteen months later—a memorable November of a memorable year. A dashing, slashing Government had been gloriously pursuing a spirited foreign policy for some time, gaily annexing a kingdom here, and a province there; light-heartedly sending our millions and our men, the one to be buried in a limbo so dark that no man could penetrate it—the other to be cut to pieces in Afghan fastnesses, or butchered by African savages who took the liberty to defend what they were foolish enough to consider their country, to which they had a right: this spirited foreign policy had for some three years been reigning glorious and triumphant abroad, with the usual results at home.

There was a depression, black and profound, over the prospects of the manufacturing and commercial world. As yet, the situation had not come to a crisis—as yet, the storm had not burst; it might be described as in a condition of gathering clouds. The first mutterings of the thunder had been heard: here some well-known bank came down with a crash, and before men's faces had recovered their colour, the alarm was sounded from another side; one heard of the downfall of some old commercial house, on whose stability those who knew would have staked their own reputations. These were the big towers; when they fell the shock resounded, and made the welkin ring. No one heeded the crowd of little cardboard fabrics, mushrooms of a day, tents pitched a week before, which came tumbling down on every side.

When the giants were tottering, one had no time to watch the destruction amongst the pigmies. The danger had not gone far enough yet to cause panic. There were pale faces and suspicious looks already, and quick interrogations, and anxious countenances flitting about amongst the crowds on 'Change ; but as yet the great merchant princes stood steady, though if all the growls that were growled over the Darkingford morning papers at each fresh glorious feat of arms, and each new crash in the commercial world, could have been collected together, they would have amounted to a tolerably ominous roar, coming, too, from the centre whose verdicts, given amidst its smoke and its grimy toilers, are said to rule England.

Where the shoe was really pinching, and that almost intolerably, was in the masses, in the working-classes, where there was darkness, and bitter poverty, and passionate discontent, and an ominously irritable temper shown.

Most of the Darkingford merchants were anxiously hoping that the Government might be signally defeated on the subject of a loan of several millions for war purposes. So far, both the Houses had appeared, with few exceptions, to be carried on with the stream, and to be blinded by the chimerical glory abroad to what was going on at home. But of late many of the large towns had been intimating to their representatives, through the emphatic vehicles of mass meetings passing strong resolutions almost without dissentient voices, that they were tired of what one popular orator denominated 'Government fireworks for which the people had to pay.' It was hoped that in the course of some important divisions which were expected to take place that this temper outside would be shown to the Ministry, who must either moderate their zeal for British interests abroad, or—go out, and let the Opposition go through the same process of a triumphant entrance into power, a gradually dwindling majority, and a final exit without pride and without distinction. On the outside view of it, one wonders how rational men are to be found to go so often through the sorry performance.

In the meantime Darkingford was in a state of commercial gloom befitting its name. Amongst the poor there was bitter poverty and pinching; amongst the better-off there was here and there a breakdown and bankruptcy; but on the whole a sort of reckless playing with the danger, for never had there been a gayer winter—so everyone said—never more entertainments and amusements more abundantly attended. Never, said some observers, had the string of carriages been so long at the doors of theatres and concert-rooms. Others, who looked a little deeper, might have replied that never had private hospitality been so scant; one may go to many concerts and theatres for a quarter of the money which it costs to give one big ball or rout or dinner-party; and many Darking-ford tradesmen, with rueful faces, could have attested to the shortcomings in this direction.

The house in Queen Street, where Margaret Hankinson and Peril lived together, had abated nothing of its usual order, for the reason that nothing could well have been more simple than that order.

Peril sat reading one afternoon by the light of a lamp, lifting her head now and then, and looking at the timepiece. She was alone, and she seemed to expect some one or something.

The street was a quiet one, but at last she heard wheels. A carriage stopped be-

fore the door, and very soon afterwards
Margaret Hankinson stood in the room.
She looked very much older, there was no
doubt, for her eighteen months' business and
other experiences. There was gravity and
anxiety in her face now, as she stood by
the table and unfastened her sealskin slowly.

'Well?' said Peril.

'Well, the vote has been given for short
time.'

'All of you?'

'Most of us. There are one or two who
mean to hold out. I should have liked to
hold out too, for the sake of the people. It
is pitiful, with winter coming on so fast—indeed it is here to-night, if ever it was—but I
dared not risk it. If it had been my own
business I would have done, and trusted to
Providence, or whatever it is that sees to
things.'

'My impression is that things are not

" seen to," as you call it, at all,' said Peril, with a little curl of her lip. ' There's a little conceited creature called man more peculiarly incapable of taking care of himself and others than any other created thing, because he knows just enough to prevent him from seeing how ignorant he is, and the whole universe is committed to his keeping. That's how things are "seen to"!'

' What a fine piece of cynical philosophy! Seated over a good fire, with a novel in your hand, it is so easy to spin out phrases like that, and roll them off, and they sound fine,' said Margaret, laying her jacket aside. ' If you had been with me this afternoon—there was just one other woman besides myself—in the midst of an assemblage of the most rough-hewn, hard-headed, blunt, uncivil, clever sort of men you ever saw together, you would have felt that woman is ignorant, whatever man may be.'

'Didn't you feel rather proud—you are twenty-nine—a young woman of twenty-nine standing there, on an equality with any of them, the representative of one of the greatest firms in all the lot of them ?'

'Proud! good gracious !' said Margaret ; but there was a little flutter round her lips which told that she was not altogether indifferent to the position she had filled at the meeting of employers which had been called to consider what would be the best way to meet and tide over the present most serious depression in their trade—that of spinning yarn, and also of weaving cotton cloth.

'Did you say anything ?' asked Peril.

'Certainly not, except to give my vote when called upon. The other lady did. She was a Mrs. Dobson, of Shawfield. I believe she has two immense factories, which she managed, after her husband died, for her son, her only child. Just when he came of age,

he died too. And they say that, to keep
herself going at all, and to fight her grief, she
kept on this work, and now it is second nature
to her.   She is a harsh, hard specimen,
speaks with a broad Lancashire accent, and
she is one of those who mean to go on with
full time for the present.   She got a little out
of order, denouncing the Government in no
measured terms.   I must say I agreed with
every word that she said ; but I thought it
best to hold my peace.   Then I had to go to
the office and see Robert Marsden, and tell
him about serving the notice, and then I came
home.'

'Where you mean to stay, I suppose ?'

'No, I don't.   I shall just sit and worry
about this business if I stop at home ; that's
where it seems to me that men have the pull
over us in these things.   They can put them
away when they leave their offices.'

'Well, I heard Mr. Whitworth saying, the

other day, that some of his happiest strokes of business had been hit upon out of office hours. But never mind. *You* would worry. What then ?'

'Oh, I shall go to the concert. It's this new thing ; this " Faust," of Berlioz. I always go to hear anything that has any connection with " Faust." You must come too.'

' I did not think of it.'

'Oh yes, you must. And we must get dressed at once, and have dinner, for it begins half an hour earlier. It is long, they say.'

'Long, is it ? Oh dear!' said Peril, little knowing to what she was going. But she saw that Margaret's mind was far more full of anxiety than she would own, and that she was bent upon going to the concert in order to drive this anxiety away, for a time at least.

Peril would have done anything for her,

for Margaret had taken her with a strong
hand and pulled her out of her morbid
gloom and despair, and had made a new
creature of her—understanding her, sympa-
thizing with her, and, at the same time,
reproving her and putting her straight in a
manner that no one else had done.   Peril had
adored Mrs. Trelawney; she still cherished
a great fondness for her, enhanced, perhaps,
by the distance that was between them; but
Mrs. Trelawney's nature was in every possible
way a smaller and narrower one than that of
Margaret Hankinson.   Her views of doing
good to Peril were bounded by the idea of
keeping her money in good hands, and marrying her into a county family—'making a lady
of her,' as it might be vulgarly expressed.
Margaret had had another aim—she had
striven to make a *woman* of her—and she
had undoubtedly wrought a great change in
her in the right direction.   There were few

topics which they had not discussed, even to the separation between Peril and Lawford. Margaret had said :

'It is not often that the sinning party can make the first advances; generally it is the one who forgives that has to hold out a hand. But I can quite see that he could never do that, at least except under *most* extraordinary circumstances.'

'Under none, that I can see. He never wishes to see me again. If he had made a mistake about me I might agree with you; but you see he didn't. I was what he said. I had done the thing that made him leave me.'

'Yes!' said Margaret, as if that did not convey much meaning to her mind.

'You don't mean,' said Peril, for whom the subject seemed to have a fascination, 'that you would ever advise *me* to have the presumption to address *him* ?'

'If a proper opportunity offered, I should say you ought certainly to express your contrition to him.'

'That would be a mockery. Besides, I do not believe I shall ever see him again. I have no doubt he has gone to South Africa with his sister. If I had not behaved like a madwoman, and a bad woman too, he could have gone to Australia to look after Hugh, instead of your having to pay a stranger, who will not do it half so well, and who, I am persuaded, is just lingering on and letting you give him money, and doing nothing.'

'I have every confidence in my agent,' said Margaret, repressing either a smile or a look of pain; it is difficult, sometimes, to distinguish between the two.

This evening, as they were going upstairs to dress, a letter was put into Peril's hands.

'From Wiswell. Why, it is Uncle Wistar's writing,' she said.

' My dear Niece Peril,

'For the last three weeks I have been feeling a very old man, and have been laid up with lumbago into the bargain. I feel very much like a farm machine that has got too rusty for any oiling to do any more good to it; only that's a bad comparison, because, thank the Lord, I shall have worn out, not rusted, when my time comes. But this is to say that, if you are in good health, as I hope, and have a little leisure, it would gladden an old man, and do him much good, to see ye. It's perhaps not for very long that he would detain you from your more congenial friends. My back is so bad I can say no more. Let me hear from ye.

'Your loving uncle,

'Geo. Wistar.'

'I shall go to-morrow, without any loss of time,' said Peril, with a rush of compunction at the thought of the lonely old man who had been so good to her, and whom she had neglected, because she feared to go within twenty miles of Wiswell Grange. 'I need not send him word,' she repeated within herself; 'I will go.'

And with this resolution she set off with Margaret to the concert.

CHAPTER II.

BITTER-SWEET.

WHATEVER may be the opinion of connoisseurs as to the merits or demerits of the 'Faust' of Berlioz, its claims to be a classical composition in the sense in which Beethoven's Symphonies and Handel's Oratorios are classical, there can be no doubt that to anyone at all sensitive to musical and emotional influences, the first hearing of it is a revelation, and one which seems to be made in a crash of fire and thunder. It effectually answered Margaret Hankinson's purpose in going to hear it; it conveyed her far away from herself and all her everyday troubles. To Peril it was a great deal more. She sat motionless and absorbed—her great eyes fixed, certainly, upon the performers, but not by any means seeing them. She listened ; she was grasped and shaken by the stream of mystic philosophy, the torrent of fiery passion, the cynicism in melody of Mephistopheles ; all her nerves were strung up to a pitch of intense excitement. 'Faust' deals with problems which appeal to us all, both high and low, vulgar and refined ; there is no phase of life, no secret of passion, which it does not touch upon ; its magic is universal, and, if the public verdict is anything to go by, it was Wolfgang Goethe who has best understood how to manipulate these secrets and this magic, and how to present them in the strangest and most fascinating guise.

Friends came up and talked and shook hands in the interval. Peril did not heed them. She sat absorbed in what she had heard, and studying the score they had brought with them, to see what was coming next. In a kind of dream she heard it all to the end; and rose, when Margaret rose, and was vaguely conscious that some one found their carriage for them and handed them into it, and that they drove away.

'Well,' observed Margaret, 'it has been a great success, without doubt. It seems to me the most wonderful thing I ever heard.'

'Seems? It is!' said Peril, in whose ears was still resounding, with its weird and rocking melody, the fantastic serenade of Mephistopheles:

> 'Dear Cath'rine, why
> To the door of thy lover
> Drawest thou nigh?
> Why there timidly hover?
> Ah, sweet maiden, beware!
> Come away! Do not enter!
> It were folly to venture.'

'What does it all mean?' she repeated aloud. 'It does not explain anything, but it seems to lift a corner of a veil, or a curtain, and show you glimpses of such abysses underneath and behind! It makes one wonder what one is walking upon, whither one is going. And you may say what you like, Margaret; it does show that things are left to chance. They are not "seen to" at all.'

'I will discuss it with you to-morrow, with pleasure,' said Margaret, laughing. 'It has made quite a different impression upon me. It was not to be expected, I suppose, that you and I would understand it alike.'

The carriage stopped before their door, and they went into the hall.

'Letters—and a telegram!' exclaimed Margaret, snatching them from the hall-table; 'from Mr. Lawford——'

'What!' gasped Peril, coming nearer to

her, with a sudden feeling of giddiness and wonder.

' From — oh — Liverpool — Hugh — what does it—is it possible ?'

' I'm very sorry to startle you, Margaret,' said a man's voice, and a man's figure emerged from the dining-room ; ' but I thought you would get my telegram before——'

' Oh, Hugh !' sobbed Margaret, and, indeed, the cheerful voice of Hugh had broken over the last syllables. He had opened his arms ; they had both forgotten every created thing except themselves—every feeling except the overwhelming one of joy at being united again.

With a feeling which overpowered her, and made her feel as if she would suffocate, Peril looked on for a moment, and saw how Margaret sprang to her lover's arms, and how his embrace seemed to swallow her up and cover her, and hold her as if he would never let her go again. They heeded her not, and saw her not. She heard him whisper something that sounded like 'Forgive!' She could bear it no more, but hurried swiftly away from them, with her heart in a tumult and a turmoil, to her room.

She had tried hard to discipline and subdue herself, but, at one-and-twenty, one must be a strange bloodless creature to have no sense of strength and youth, no power of resentment or jealousy, never to speak of love and passion. Margaret's probation was over, and it was she who would come forth triumphant from the furnace. She had done her work bravely—had earned her lover's worship in every way—her path would be smooth, her way open before her, for the future. And Peril felt neither envy nor regret in the consummation. It was well; it was just and meet that it should be so. She did not grudge her one kiss or one caress, or one word of adoration; but the sight of their happiness had made her feel more of an outcast than ever. If it had been Paul, for instance, who had come out of that room, what would have happened? She would have had nothing to do but cast down her eyes, that she might not see the blank coldness in his— and pass on, just as she had done now. The idea grew almost unbearably painful; one gleam of light, and one only, crossed her mind—the recollection of her uncle's letter, and that to-morrow she could get away from all this.

A knock at her door, followed by the entrance of Margaret, looking—was it really the same Margaret who had come in from the concert, looking almost middle-aged, with care and business in every line of every feature? This was a girl, radiant with happiness, and transformed in every way.

'Peril, I am afraid we made a sad exhibi-
tion of ourselves!' said this new Margaret, in
a soft, happy voice, which seemed to tremble
between laughter and tears. 'I do not
wonder that you fled, horror-struck. But I
had been in such suspense for weeks, waiting
to hear from Mr. Lawford, whether——'

'You spoke of Mr. Lawford before,' said
Peril, in an excited voice. 'What do you
mean? What have you and Hugh to do
with Mr. Lawford?'

'Come down, and you shall hear all about
it from him,' said Margaret, taking her hand,
and leading her downstairs. Peril followed,
her unwillingness overcome by the strong
spell exercised by Lawford's name, and the
promise that she should hear something
about him. It was of this she was thinking
as they entered the parlour, but for a
moment this died out of her mind as her
eyes fell upon Hugh, looking a little older,

very much bronzed, taller, broader, handsomer than ever, leaning with his back against the mantelpiece, just in the spot on which Paul had stood on that afternoon which she recalled, with hot shame, every day of her life. And when she saw him, there rushed into Peril's mind the recollection of the letter she had written to him, and of the answer he had sent to her—of his determined resolution not to abate one jot of the punishment she had had to endure for her fault—of the recklessness with which he had behaved, and the selfishness, such it appeared to her. With the sight of his figure came back the remembrance of all those miserable days at Great North Street when she had loved him—or thought she had—and before she had known Paul. If all had been right now between her and Paul, she could have met Hugh with equanimity. As it was, Margaret had per-

haps done better to let her stay in her room
—for to-night, at least.

Her face was white ; her great eyes were
dry and not very gentle-looking as Margaret
led her into the room, and she fixed them
upon Hugh without speaking, while the
flood of bitter and angry recollections rushed
into her mind. He cared for Margaret—that,
to Peril, appeared now to be about the only
title to her esteem which he possessed.
And Hugh was not pleasantly moved by
the apparition of his cousin. Margaret had
forgiven, and condoned, and smiled upon him ;
but when he saw Peril, his conscience smote
and smote—he was not fond of asking forgiveness, and he had done it several times
already this night. Margaret suddenly felt,
as she saw them look at each other, that
these were two antagonistic elements which
she would have done better not to bring into
collision. It was now, however, too late to

draw back. She put the best face upon the matter, and in a voice which was not without a tone of warning, said:

'Hugh, here is Peril. She has to go away early to-morrow, so she must hear your news to-night.'

'Peril—I had somehow forgotten that you would be here. This is a meeting quite like old times, isn't it? It only wants Aunt Agatha to make it complete.'

He could hardly have made a more unfortunate remark, as he instantly felt. The name of Mrs. Robson, indeed, was one which it was scarcely seemly to utter within Peril's hearing.

'Forgotten?' said Peril, coldly and drily. 'I don't see how you could ever know, much less forget that I was here.'

'I have known for long enough. Paul told me.'

'Paul!' she repeated, with a flash of her

eyes. ' I want to know the meaning
of——'

' Dear Peril,' said Margaret earnestly, ' I
never told you because I did not want to
disturb you. It is Mr. Lawford who has
been to Australia to see after this wretched
young man. He came to me in my trouble,
you know, just after my father's death, and
offered to go. And I was only too thankful
for his goodness.'

' And you did not tell me,' said Peril,
darkly and haughtily. ' I call that most
extraordinary conduct, from a friend.'

There was an embarrassed silence. Margaret could not find it in her heart to tell
Peril, before Hugh, that Paul had stipulated
expressly that Peril was to know nothing
about the arrangement. It was again an
instance of being unprovided for the unexpected.

Margaret had heard repeatedly from Lawford, and so long as things took their normal course, had preserved her presence of mind and kept silence.   But, as she truly said, she had been in a state of strained suspense for many weeks now.   Lawford's last letter had told her not to be too much elated if he said he thought he had a clue to Hugh's fate; he believed he was on the road for finding out whether he was alive or dead.   More he could not tell her, but he thought it best to let her know that.

Day by day she had waited, in an agony of suspense and fear ; and no letter had come, and her heart had begun to give way within her.   The letter which she had found on the hall-table had been from Lawford, to say that he had found Hugh, who had gone with the exploring expedition, not meaning to accompany it far, but had been prevented from returning by difficulties of various kinds.   He had gone through severe hardships with his companions, and had seen many of them dying around him. Then he had resolved, in spite of all expostulations, to turn back and try to fight his way to Melbourne alone, with his gun, and on his own feet. The result had been that between fever and starvation he had been prostrate, and picked up nearly dying by some friendly bush-folk, who had nursed and doctored him in their own way. He had got better as well as he could, his youth and strength triumphing over disadvantages, the greatest of which was his wild and passionate anxiety to get back into civilized regions and relieve the horrible anxiety and suspense about him in which he knew that Margaret must have been plunged. He had set off before he was properly recovered, alone, and had naturally been attacked again by illness ; and it was during this last bout that Lawford had found him, and come to him from Melbourne.

Paul had written off to Margaret (the letter which had arrived this night), telling her of Hugh's illness, promising that he should write himself as soon as he was able for it, and saying he should bring him home as soon as he was fit to be moved.

The letter had been posted; and then Hugh, in a brief interval of strength, had insisted with passionate determination upon setting off then and there in the very vessel which brought his letter, saying he would never be well while he was in that cursed country, but that the voyage, he was sure, would set him up.

Although with many misgivings, Paul had yielded, and had him conveyed to the vessel.

Hugh's prognostication had proved right. The voyage had restored him in a marvellously short time to something like health and strength, though even now he was lank and haggard, and stooped somewhat in his carriage.

Knowing that the letter would arrive no sooner than himself, Hugh had, immediately on arriving at Liverpool, telegraphed to Margaret to say he should be with her that night. He thrust aside Paul's suggestions that he should substitute ' to-morrow ' for ' to-night,' saying that he would not sleep a wink ; and he was sure she would not, knowing that they were so near to each other and yet separated.

Letter and telegram had come almost together, and Hugh had speedily followed them—and all had found Margaret absent.

This was the tale which Hugh now, with somewhat scant details, eked out by Margaret's interruptions, repeated to Peril, who listened to it intently, hearkening all the time for Paul's name, and hearing little of the rest.

'Now he is back, and all is well,' said Margaret, when he had done.

'If it had not been for Paul,' said Hugh, 'I don't believe I should ever have been back again. He looked after me like—well, like a friend. Brothers are not always so brotherly as that.'

'By the way,' said Margaret, suddenly putting the question which Peril had been burning to ask, but would rather have died than done so, 'what did Mr. Lawford do? Did he come to Darkingford too?'

'He took train straight off to London, to join his sister and his boy,' said Hugh. 'He seemed awfully impatient to be off.'

'Is he going to stay there?'

'Don't know, I'm sure. He is awfully reserved about his private affairs. And it was not for me to ask.'

'I hope he will write to me directly. Did he give you no address? I want to shake hands with him, and tell him I shall love him as long as I live.'

'Oh, I've a plan about him,' said Hugh, with a nod, bespeaking much inward satisfaction.

Peril felt almost choking with grief and indignation. It was perfectly evident that Hugh had not only accepted his changed fortunes, but had managed to become thoroughly reconciled to them. Her sacrifice had been effectual enough. Why, she could not help asking herself with passionate emotion, had he not been frank and modest, and met her half-way, and rendered that sacrifice unnecessary. She had made it, had wrecked her life and her happiness in making it, and he gaily took it, and said nothing about it. And he had 'a plan about Paul.' She clenched her hands together, feeling as if she must shriek. The agonizing part of it was that she had no right to gainsay him ; he

had a right to have a plan for rewarding the
man who had saved him from the jaws of
death, and that man had a right to enter into
the plan if it seemed good to him. She had
for ever forfeited the right to have any say
in the matter. She had offered Paul money
to rid her of him ; he had refused her money,
and given her her freedom, with some strong
expressions which retained to this moment
their primitive power to scorch and wither
her up whenever she recalled them. These
people were happy, were light-hearted ; they
had got through their troubles, and were
already beginning to make plans for the
future. But would they have got so far if it
had not been for her ? She could not sit
still under this silent storm of feeling that
was going on in her, and she got up with
flaming eyes and compressed lips.

'I am glad to have heard your story,' she
said, speaking to him as to some stranger

who had been recounting his adventures. 'It is very interesting ; the only drawback about it is, that it seems to me things *might* have been settled without all this anxiety and trouble if——'

'Don't let us go into that, Peril,' he said impulsively. 'I may have been stupid and obstinate. But if I had it to do over again, I should do it. Shake hands, and let bygones be bygones.'

'When they *are* bygones,' she answered, in a tone of indescribable bitterness, 'no one will be better pleased than I shall to let them sleep. You seem able easily to forget. I cannot, and——'

'Peril,' he said earnestly, 'Lawford told me all that you had done, and——'

'So I perceive. As Margaret told you, I am going away to-morrow, and I wish to be spared all details of business, except what relates just to my own, and no other. Fortunately, she has had the management of it all. I had nothing to do with it. I have done what I intended to do,' she added, walking up to Hugh, and looking at him defiantly. 'You were in the wrong when you calculated upon defeating me. You might have knòwn that I do not submit for an hour to carrying anything like a stain with me. If you had chosen, you might have made it very easy for me. As it is, I have carried my purpose through; but as for my happiness, or the rest of my life——'

She shrugged her shoulders, and there was a cynic indifference about the gesture which made him feel intensely uncomfortable. Indeed, the whole scene made him uncomfortable. It was in any case unpleasant, when you were just in the first glow and triumph of return to life, and to love, and to happiness, to be confronted by sneers and jeers, and told that if you had been less selfish you need never have strayed from those paths. But it was ten times more unpleasant when you were forced to feel that the accusations contained more than a grain of truth.

He was impatient of such things; he did not want to have to submit to them, and he took upon himself to point out to Peril how the difficulty might be obviated.

'Your happiness,' he said, 'need not be destroyed. I don't know what is the quarrel between you and Paul, but I'm sure of this, that——'

'At your peril you mention him to me!' she suddenly cried, turning upon him in a perfect blaze of anger, with eyes flashing, hands clenched, and passion in every tone. 'You are the last person who has the right to speak his name to me. What is between us is between us; and if you dare to meddle with it, I will never speak to you again. Margaret,' she added, turning to the other, with a sudden and complete change of manner, with a weariness in her voice and an apathy in her tones which wrung Margaret's heart, ' I am sorry I came downstairs. I will go away now. If I have said anything to hurt you, you must forgive me, like the good woman that you are. I have a great many sad thoughts in my mind, and no end of follies to repent of—but I am so glad that you are happy !'

She put her arms round Margaret's neck, and laid her head upon her shoulder, and kissed her many times ; and then saying, ' Good-night ; I shall be busy to-morrow, for the train leaves early, and it is late now ;' she kissed her again, and went out of the room, without bestowing a look upon Hugh.

' What is there wrong between Lawford and her ?' asked the latter. ' I never fancied it was anything to speak of. I said to Paul, after he told me that he was married to her,

that they were treating me a lot better than
I deserved, to part so soon ; and I wondered
that Peril consented to let him go, as she
wasn't generally very ready to do such
things. And all he said was, that Peril had
made it the object of her life to get this
matter settled, and he was wishful that she
should be satisfied.'

Margaret told him briefly enough the facts
of the case. Hugh felt his complacency and
satisfaction with things in general falling very
low as he heard the tale.

'Poor Peril!' he observed. 'She always
took everything so hard. I wonder if it will
ever get put straight ?'

CHAPTER III.

WISWELL AGAIN.

'AH, lass, I'm fain to see thee.—fain, fain, I am !'

Such had been the old man's greeting to his niece, when she had walked, totally unexpected by him, into his room, on the dripping, dark November evening—that following the one of Hugh's return to Darkingford. His joy and pleasure touched her deeply. She was glad she had come, and there was a little glow of excitement about it all at first, which speedily died away and left everything flavourless. It seemed to Peril as if she had got back into the old

groove, with an exactitude of sameness and
narrowness which had something ghastly in
it—the groove, that is, as it had formerly
been, before Katty or Humphrey or Paul
had come to Wiswell—in the days when she
had been in a way enjoying rest and thankfulness in the society of her old uncle and
the companionship of the Trelawneys. Nay,
even this last had come back. She had
found Mr. Trelawney sitting with Mr.
Wistar on her arrival; he had greeted her
in a way which showed that neither time,
nor absence, nor the things which had
happened, had made the slightest difference
in his feelings for her. The next day he
came to her, with a message from his wife
—would she come up and see her in the
afternoon? Peril accepted the spirit of the
overture—consented, and they met again.
Nothing had been said about past events.
Only Mr. Trelawney, with an odd twinkle

in his eyes, had told Peril that she would be glad to hear of Stephen Harkland's happy engagement to a certain fashionable beauty, who was said also to be—and the two perhaps do not go so often together—a 'very nice girl.' Not a word was breathed by either of the Trelawneys to Peril on the subject of her marriage, though it was, of course, known to them. She had told her uncle, who had told them. She could only gather from their behaviour to her that they chose to continue their friendship with her, and ignore all dangerous subjects. This conduced to make the situation outwardly similar to what it had been before. Inwardly, Peril knew how different it was, and how, so it seemed to her, she had spent passion and action, and had made vain and futile struggles, and wasted a vast amount of emotion, with no result but a blank, both inward and outward.

She got a letter from Margaret, not very
long after her arrival, fuller of herself than
Margaret's epistles usually were—full of the
relief she felt at her freedom from business
toils; full of Hugh's quickness and clever-
ness, and of how everything was now going
right, and how they were going to be
married, very quietly, directly after Christ-
mas. Paul's name was not mentioned. Peril
stifled her feelings of bitterness, sat down
and forced herself to write a sisterly letter
to Margaret—in which the feeling at any
rate was real, if the expression of it were a
little forced.

She wondered secretly where Paul was,
and what he was doing. Her thoughts were
more occupied with him than ever; and
here, in Wiswell, everything reminded her
of him. She could not escape from his
silent, invisible presence. The upland roads
along which they had strolled on summer

evenings, with Humphrey and Katty; the broad yellow sands; the edge of the sea beside which they had paced, watching the crisply curling waves; the deserted church-yard, which now she literally dared not enter; and, most of all, the equally deserted Grange itself, which she passed on some excuse or other daily, lingering about its gates, straining her ear to catch perchance some last echo of the pleasant voices whose cadences used to greet her there—surely they were not absolutely and for ever stilled! Nothing could possibly have been more sad, more mournful, and more desolate to look at than this same old Grange in the November weather. The sodden brown leaves lay in thick masses on the garden walks and on the grass, while from the now bare twigs and branches a kind of rainy dew seemed to distil itself, as if the very trees wept at the sad condition of the poor old

house.   Alternate storms of wind and rain
had laid low the long lank grass which lay
in matted disorder over what had been a
velvet sward.   The few autumn flowers, the
lingering asters and snap-dragons and late
roses, turned pale at the appalling prospect
which met their opening eyes.   They
sickened, withered, died, and were beaten
down to the earth, wan and shapeless.   As
for the house itself, it seemed to partake in
the universal sorrow of everything around it.
Its grey walls seemed to take a deeper and
more iron tinge ; the windows, closed and
shuttered, got dim and discoloured with
successive coatings of dust, of wet, and of
droppings from the trees.   The oaken front
door, with its sturdy iron knobs, remained
sternly shut—that door which had been wont
to stand cheerfully open, welcoming sun and
wind, rain and shine alike almost—anything
except grim and ungracious winter cold.

There was nothing fresh to see—nothing cheering; but Peril, not telling anyone of her custom, used daily to visit the entrance gates, at least, and gaze, so long as she felt herself unobserved, upon the damp and soaking avenue, and the melancholy brown front of the house. It continued to be voiceless, sightless, inarticulate, if one may use such expressions of a house; and to my mind a dwelling which is now deserted, and which one has known inhabited and full of life, takes more the appearance of a sentient thing paralyzed, than of a mere deserted structure of wood and stone.

One dank afternoon, Peril left the Rectory, where she had been sitting with Mrs. Trelawney, to go to her uncle. The old man had so far recovered that he had been lifted from his bed, and was that afternoon to be carried downstairs. His niece was determined to spend the evening with him. She had been telling Mrs Trelawney of his odd, frugal ways—of how he refused to allow himself this, that, and the other little luxury, just because he had never been in the habit of indulging in them ; and could not be brought to see that when he was ill a difference might be appropriately made. She found a pleasure in circumventing his little economies, and out of her own means providing him with the things he needed. For she was now one-and-twenty, married, and consequently in receipt of the income from the fortune which was to accrue to her under those circumstances.

Gathering up her knitting in her hand, she put her hat on her head, and her fur mantle round her shoulders ; gave Mrs. Trelawney the kiss which had again been established between them, and left the house.

Outside, she paused. She wished to go quickly to her uncle, but she had not this day paid her usual visit to the deserted lane which led up to the Grange gates. She hesitated a moment; then decided that it was a luxury she need not deny herself, since it was in itself a deep mortification—scarcely one of these sinful and sensual pleasures from which it is as well now and then to take a fast. She would not stay long, but her heart felt empty, her eyes unsatisfied, until she had looked upon the place once more and accepted its silent reproach and reproof; for that was what she read in its stillness and deathliness. It seemed to cry out to her, to look what she had done. She walked towards the lane which branched off from the high-road. It was dusk—the November twilight was rapidly deepening into night, and there was a dim, dank haze over everything. Figures and faces looked vague and magnified and mysterious through this nebulous medium; and the brown hedges and the sodden roads gave one a kind of smothered, stifled sensation.   Here was the corner of the lane—the grass and weeds which covered it, and which, as it was a private road, it did not concern the parish to remove, made it green.   Her foot had entered it; she was obviously proceeding towards the gates, when, rounding the corner, and also coming towards the house, but from the opposite direction to that from which she came, appeared the figure of a man walking rather heavily and slowly.   On his shoulder he carried a child, the sight of whose fair, frank face sent a thrill through Peril's whole being. And the man who carried him, and whose eyes suddenly fell from the child's face into which he had been looking up with a smile, and were arrested by Peril's figure—the smile died out of both face and eyes—nothing remained but blank coldness.

She scarcely breathed—she shrank involuntarily against the hedge, and averted her face, and would if she could gladly have been fifty fathoms underground. He did make a momentary pause, and then, as if recollecting himself, walked on silently, with a quicker, firmer tread; and she heard him say:

'Now, my lad, don't drop asleep before we get into the house.'

Mechanically, hardly knowing what she did, Peril found her way to Stanesacre. As she entered the house she met Mr. Trelawney, his hat in his hand, just about to leave it.

'Peril—what is the matter with you?' he asked, startled by her pale face and scared eyes.

'Mr. Trelawney—come here, I want to speak to you,' she said, drawing him into one of the empty parlours, and shutting the door. 'I have seen—not a ghost, I wish it was— I have just seen Paul and Humphrey.'

'Paul and Humphrey—what, here, in Wiswell?'

'Here, in Wiswell, going up to the Grange. Did you know of it?'

'I assure you, my child, I knew absolutely nothing of it.'

'Mr. Trelawney, will you be very kind and good, and find out why he has come, and how long he is going to stay?'

'Would not you be the more suitable person to do that, seeing——'

'Of all persons in the world, I am just the one who may not speak to him, or approach him in any way. He told me I was lower than the lowest to him, and that he would never forgive me the wrong I had done him. If I do not know about him I shall go mad. Dear, dear Mr. Trelawney, you said you were my friend, and would help me—will you not do this for me?'

'I will do what I can,' said he gravely.

'Oh, how good you are! I feel that he can only have come here because he is in trouble —there must be some strong reason to bring him back here. If he stays, I must go. I cannot remain in a place where a person lives who loathes the sight of me, and thinks me vile,' she concluded passionately.

'Would it not be best to make some advance, and show you are nothing of the kind?' he suggested. But Peril declined the very thought of such a thing.

'He was smiling up into Humphrey's face,' she said, 'and as soon as his eyes fell upon me, he seemed to turn to ice, and walked past me, as the Levites and priests passed the man who had fallen amongst thieves.'

'In that case he has done you a wrong.'

'Not one—it is I who have wronged him grievously.'

'But, my dear child, when you have done a wrong, and know that you have, it is the one indispensable first step towards putting it right, that you should go to the person you have wronged, and humbly ask forgiveness.'

'And if that other thinks your very addressing him to be a piece of unbounded presumption? No, I know how best to please him—or rather, how least to offend him—it is by keeping out of his sight and out of his way. But you will find out what I want to know, dear Mr. Trelawney?'

A slight smile crossed the rector's lips. He began to see a little more clearly, just from the very paradox into which she put her sentiments. She was to keep away from him, and out of his sight and mind, and so she would least offend him; but she must know all about him, and why he had come, and how long he was going to stay. She was bound to take no step whatever to approach him, and yet Mr. Trelawney thought he saw a gleam of light in this contradiction. He tried to reassure her; told her he would, of course, call upon Lawford if he was making any stay, and would let her know the result of his visit.

When at last Peril heard this result, her perturbation and her feeling of helplessness were even greater than they had been before. Since Lawford's arrival had been known to her, she had scarcely stirred out of the house. Her uncle still continued ill, and wanted much nursing and attention, and this served her as a pretext for remaining indoors. All her thoughts were in that lonely house, and with the two inhabitants of it. Mr. Trelawney at last told her he had seen Mr. Lawford, and had some conversation with him.

'Well?' she asked, breathlessly.

'He looks rather forlorn in that dreadful old damp house,' pursued Mr. Trelawney, watching her keenly but kindly, and purposely telling the story in a particular way, because he wished to work on her mind in a particular direction.

' He has not been in England very long.'

' No ; I know.'

' On his return from Melbourne with young Nowell he went straight to London, to see his sister and her husband. Mr. Woodfall has got a sort of agency out at the Cape for a business house in London. They set off two days after Mr. Lawford's return ; so he is left with his little boy in his charge, and he says he never knew before what a wonderful woman Mrs. Woodfall was, though he always thought no end of her !'

' Peril's lips parted ; her eyes said, ' Go on.'

' It seems,' Mr. Trelawney proceeded deliberately, 'that Mr. Lawford, having decided that there is nothing to keep him in England, or indeed to tie him anywhere— as he observed to me, there is not a soul in the wide world who wants him, except this sister and her husband—has resolved to sell his little estate here, and go out to join them.'

'Oh !' said Peril, with a kind of gasp. ' He will go out to them ?'

' Yes. He says he has not the means to push his child, and give him the education necessary to put him into a profession; he thinks he will feel it less in a country where, if the prizes are not so big, they are more equally distributed.'

'Ah ! but—when he says there is no one who wants him—I should have thought Hugh Nowell ; surely,' she said, scarcely able to control her voice, 'he does not forget that my—that Mr. Lawford saved his life, and behaved more like an elder brother to him than——'

'Oh no! It seems your cousin is most anxious that Mr. Lawford should come and take a position of trust in his works. He has urged him in every way to do so.'

'And why does he not? Why expatriate himself, and sell his estate, which I know he loves, though it is so fallen, when by a word he might have everything to make him pros-perous and happy?'

'He told me—he entered into no par-ticulars, but I said something of the same kind—at least, I ventured to suggest that I was sorry he could not see his way, for his son's sake, to do this. He replied that no doubt I should think him visionary and sentimental—he had always been noted for it—but that not long ago he had anticipated a happiness here, in this country, so great, that when the prospect of it was suddenly and arbitrarily withdrawn, almost at the moment of fruition, he had got a blow from which, in a certain way, he would never recover. He had no intention of mooning his life away, or in any way, he hoped, making a fool of himself; but it was simply intolerable to him to remain here while he could go elsewhere; and while he was very fond of Hugh Nowell, and made him heartily welcome to any trifling service he had rendered him, yet a closer connection with him would be more painful than pleasant. If there had been no other opening, he would have felt it his duty to accept his offer; as it was, he was grateful, but he declined it.'

'He will put the seas between us, and then he will be content,' said Peril to herself.

'In the meantime,' Mr. Trelawney pursued, 'he is about as uncomfortable as he well can be. He came—just like a man, my wife says: they think neither of themselves nor of anyone else—to this dreadful, damp old house, without giving warning to anyone, or writing for a servant to be sent in, or fires to be made, or anything. He and Humphrey travelled by night, and arrived early in the morning. They lighted fires,

and did things for themselves chiefly, I fancy.
He has now got the young woman in the
house who was Mrs. Woodfall's servant, and
she has reduced things into something like
order ; but not before the boy caught a bad
cold—a sort of bronchitis—and is kept in
one room, quite an invalid, poor little fellow!
Mr. Lawford diversifies his leisure by alter-
nately making expeditions on foot into Foulhaven and amusing poor Humphrey, who
does not appreciate the situation at all.
They were solemnly playing beggar-my-
neighbour when I appeared upon the scene,
and Humphrey, having lost largely, was
accusing his father of cheating, and insisted
upon seeing his cards.'

Peril forced a smile at the picture, but
her chief feeling was one of scorching humiliation and shame at the fact, which she
realized from every word of Mr. Trelawney's,
that Paul's resolution had never changed

since the day when he told her he had lost all wish to deprive her of her freedom. He was in the same mind yet. He preferred anything—to sell his patrimony, and expatriate himself and his boy, when he might have had plenty and honourable prosperity at home—rather than abide in the same country with her, who had so outraged and insulted him. The only gleam of relief in this certainty was that it was certainty; she was spared the agony and the shame of making an advance, and receiving a rebuff. Now at last her fate was quite certain and decided, and all that remained for her was to make up her mind to encounter it, and live it out as well as she could. One or two questions she still had to ask.

'When does the sale of the Grange take place?'

'Next Saturday.'

'And if he does not sell it?'

'I think there is no danger of that.
Stephen Harkland has often said his father
would like it.'

'Stephen Harkland!' repeated Peril indignantly.

'Well, he could not have a better or more
liberal purchaser.'

'No, perhaps not.   Well?'

'And there are others.   It is not bad land,
and would be a very profitable speculation
for some one of these squires or people.   He
is only waiting so long, in order that the sale
might be advertised in the *Foulhaven
Courier*.   He will be off as soon as he can
afterwards.'

She moved her head assentingly, but
looked abstracted.   Mr. Trelawney said:

'They say it is ill to interfere between
man and wife; all I can say is, you know I
am your friend, and as your friend I advise
you to put on your things, and walk into the

Grange parlour, and say to him that you have come to stay with him, and look after Humphrey. You would clear away every difficulty at a stroke.'

She shook her head, as he saw, with firm conviction that no such simple and primitive measure was available ; and Mr. Trelawney left her in a state of uncertainty as to whether he had done good or made mischief.

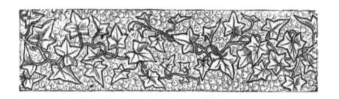

CHAPTER IV.

LOST AND FOUND.

WISWELL GRANGE, with all the lands, outhouses, and farm-buildings belonging to it, was sold. It had fetched the sum of two thousand five hundred pounds—at least five hundred more, said the agent to Paul, than he had expected to get for it.

'Who has bought it?' asked Paul.

This was on the Monday afternoon following the sale. Paul had gone down to Foulhaven, to the agent's office, in order that the sale might be ratified, as he had expressed a wish that it might be settled as soon as possible.

'I don't know,' said the man. 'Markers, the solicitors, were bidding for some one. They could tell you, if you prefer to know.'

'I certainly do,' said he. 'I'll go there and ask, and come back to you here.'

He was slightly acquainted with Mr. Marker, an urbane gentleman of the old school, who gave him a private interview at once.

'Do you object to tell me for whom you bought in Wiswell Grange, because I don't care to ratify the sale without knowing who has got it?'

'Certainly, my dear Mr. Lawford. Our client wished her name to be concealed only in case she did not get it. We bought the Grange for Mrs. Lawford.'

'Then,' said Paul, almost without a moment's pause, 'I must take a day to con-

sider about it. I do not know whether I
shall sell it to Mrs. Lawford. You will
oblige me by considering this matter private,
Mr. Marker.'

'Certainly, Mr. Lawford. Good - afternoon to you—a wet November, isn't it ?'

'Yes,' said Paul briefly, putting up his
umbrella, and going back to the agent's.
He told him he would try to see him again
the next day, and without further explaining
himself, left the office, and prepared for his
trudge home.

The *contretemps* was one which annoyed
and disturbed him excessively. He was
occupied in a debate, as he toiled along the
dreary and heavy miles which lay between
Foulhaven and Wiswell as to which would
answer his purpose the best—which would
most strongly show his resolution—to send
word to the agent that he declined to sell
to Mrs. Lawford, or to ratify the contract,

and appear to ignore personal feelings in the
matter altogether.

Since he had met her that afternoon, his
one object had been to get away from this
place—from the neighbourhood, and everything connected with her. His peace of
mind demanded it. He, as well as she, was
haunted, and pursued by ghosts, so long as
he remained here; and he had found the
idea that he might at any time encounter
her again, very disturbing to his mental
equilibrium; it upset him, and troubled him,
and took away all sense of peace or tran-
quillity. But by the time he arrived at
the Grange, when it was nearly dark, he
had decided to let the sale stand as it was.
It made no real difference. It need not
alter anything. Even if he declined to sell
it to her, the only result would be a scandal
worse than the present one; would let all
these agents and solicitors see their quarrel,

and in the end she might buy it again from some other person. If she wanted it she would have it. Self-communion told him that the most sensible and the most dignified course was to let it go—let it stand as it was. And then, of course, he began to ask himself:

'Why did she want it? Why had she bought it?'

'Oh,' said Paul to himself, 'because—because she is perversity itself, and such a trick would give her more pleasure than anything else.'

Of course it would. Anything bizarre and perverse she delighted in. How irritating she had always proved herself with regard to him—and how unutterably flat and dull life had been ever since he had parted from her! Not that he had the slightest or faintest intention of altering or trying to reverse that parting verdict. She had

proved to him then so very plainly that
she felt not a spark of love for him, that,
so he had often told himself—and, indeed,
so he was convinced in his inmost soul—the
man who could of his own will make any
advances after such a rebuff—such an un-
equivocal, undisguised slap in the face, would
be worse than a fool—he would be a poltroon
to boot, would deserve to have been so
treated. No, he would call on Harrowby,
the agent, to-morrow, get it all settled, and
go off to London with Humphrey by the
night train.

He walked up to the house door, and was
somewhat disappointed not to see his boy's
face glued against the window-pane, looking
out for his coming, as it usually had been.
He hoped Humphrey had not been rambling
about the damp old house, and made his
cold worse. So thinking, he entered, and
while he was divesting himself of his damp

overcoat, turned his face with a half smile
in the direction of the parlour, expecting to
hear the voice from within—for Humphrey
was forbidden to leave one room, except
when, with a shawl over his head, he was
carried to his bedroom.

' Are you asleep, boy ?' asked his father,
opening the door, and going into the room.
He was met by a black, blank chillness.
The fire was out—the room was empty.
Was it empty ? Was he not asleep on the
sofa, while that fool of a girl had neglected
to mend the fire, and probably thrown him
back for days ? Two steps to the sofa, a
rapid tossing about of its shawls and rugs
convinced him that his son was not there.
Two strides more took him, with his heart
beating thickly from some indefinable reason,
back into the passage, where he called upon
' Anna !' in tones such as that respectable
maidservant had certainly never heard from

her courteous master before. Did she hear now ? There was no answer. There was a weird, uncanny silence over the whole house ; he could hear the eight-day clock ticking loudly on the stairs—then a blast of cold, raw air from the kitchen regions informed him that the back door was wide open. He strode thither ; the fire burnt ; but no human soul gave any life to the scene.

'Anna!' he called again, stalking out into the yard ; and in more peremptory tones still he reiterated his call.

From the lane at the back, flying through the dusk, came a young woman's figure ; with face white and scared, and wringing her hands wildly.

'Oh, sir! oh, sir!' was all she found to say.

'What's the meaning of this? Where is Humphrey ?'

'Oh, Mr. Lawford, sir! I don't *know !*'

The voice rose into a wail of fear and alarm, and the announcement was followed by a loud sobbing.

'You don't know! what do you mean, girl? You must have seen or heard him if he went out.'

'Indeed, and I never did, sir. I was on my knees, scouring my kitchen as hard as ever I could, and never noticed how time went, when I looks up and says to myself, "Lawks! it's half-past four. I wonder if Master Humphrey has gone to sleep? it's time he had his milk and bread." And I only stopped to put the milk on the fire— there 'tis in that pan, burnt to a cinder—and I ran into the parlour, and he was gone. I've hunted high and low, and screamed and called, I have; and I think he's been stolen. It's a lonely road, and there's a deal of tramps.'

'Stolen—what rubbish!' he said, angrily;

' he has more likely put on his hat and gone out because he was dull ; and if he has, he's done for. Do you go—stop—let me see myself if he is anywhere about.'

With which, calling upon Humphrey's name, he investigated every nook and cranny of the house that was large enough to secrete a mouse, and every corner of every shed and outhouse. Humphrey was most decidedly in none of them. Having made himself quite certain of this, Paul, controlling his alarm as well as he could, and remembering his child's favourite haunts, bade Anna accompany him to the village, that they might inquire in every house. Through the mirk evening they plodded ; it did not take very long to rouse all Wiswell, and in all Wiswell there was no trace to be found of Humphrey Lawford. The thing was so impossible that he felt as if he must laugh at it—so real that fear and something like a sob shook him, when, after an hour's eager searching, they were no nearer success than before.

'I shall go and see Mr. Trelawney,' observed Paul. 'Do you go in and light a good fire, and have something hot for him to drink. Mr. Trelawney may be able to suggest something.'

'Please, sir,' suggested Anna timidly, 'Master Humphrey used to go a deal to Stanesacre—could he have strayed there, do you think?'

'No, I am quite sure he has not,' said her master. 'Do you suppose, if he had, that they would keep him there all this time, without sending me word?'

'Why, no, sir, I suppose not,' said Anna, shrinking back into silence; for though she, in common with every gossip in the place, knew that there was something serious amiss between Lawford and this young woman who it seemed was Mrs. Lawford, yet neither she nor anyone else would have ventured to breathe any allusion to the quarrel.

'Go home quickly,' he said to her, 'and do as I have told you, while I go to Mr. Trelawney's. It is just possible he may have gone there.'

He knew in his own mind that it was about as impossible a thing as anything that could be conceived ; but he wished Anna to be out of the way, and as soon as she was, he turned off to Stanesacre. Despite his repudiation of the theory that Humphrey might have gone there, he knew it was within the range of possibility that such a thing might have happened. He could ask at the door—a servant could give him an answer. So he went up the walk and knocked.

He did not know whether to be most angry or most relieved when, on the door being opened, he heard Humphrey's voice in a peal of laughter, from one of the parlours. 'He is here, then!' he exclaimed, forgetting everything else in his excitement. 'I never heard of anything so inconsiderate as not to send me word. Please to tell my little boy that I am here, waiting for him.'

'Won't you step in, sir?'

'No, I cannot. I am wet through—I will wait here in the hall. Tell him to come instantly, as I have no time to waste.'

As the maid was going towards the parlour door, which stood just ajar, it was opened. Peril—she, and no other—came forth and closed it after her.

'Mr. Lawford's come for his little boy, ma'am.'

'Yes. You can go, Mary. Will you come in here?' said Peril to him, putting her hand on the handle of the other door.

'I would prefer to wait here, thank you,' he said, coldly. 'I have been looking for

Humphrey for more than an hour, in the greatest anxiety—you must excuse me if I decline to wait or to sit down.'

' Oh, he is not going back to the Grange to-night,' said she, looking at him with an expression which he could have sworn was akin to a smile. She opened the door, and moved her hand towards the interior. ' I beg as a great favour that you will come in—I want just to say something about Humphrey.'

Lawford looked at her, and as he looked, her old witchery threw its spell over him stronger than ever. What did she want now — what freak, half-impish, half-genial, had she in contemplation? Common sense bade him go, while it was time. Something else suggested that that would look very much as if he were afraid of her—which, of course, he was not. He had shaken off her bonds long ago. A hard feeling crossed

his mind : did she want a few more home-
truths—to hear again what he was going to do
with his life ? did she imagine she had any
power or any influence over him ? Good! He
would go with her, and show her her mistake.
Without a word he went into the parlour,
and she followed him, and closed the door.

They stood together ; he as if he were on
the point of departure, his hat in his hand,
waiting for her to speak. She clasped her
hands together, and looked at him, half-
audacious, half-afraid.

' I fear you have had a sad fright about
Humphrey ?'

' Yes, I have. And I must repeat that I
wish to take him away.'

' This would, of course, be the last place in
which you would think of looking for him ?'

' It would, because I explained to him
when we came to Wiswell, that I did not
wish him to come here.'

'So he said, but I persuaded him to disobey you.'

'*You* persuaded him! Have you——'

'I saw you on your way to Foulhaven as I was driving out of it this afternoon; so I drove to the Grange, and while your maid was scouring floors and singing hymns at the top of her voice, I—stole Humphrey.'

'Stole him?'

'Yes. And I had to tell stories in order to get him to come. I said I had met you, and that you had said I was to call and fetch him here, and you would call in in the evening— which you have done, you see,' said Peril, with a look, partly demure, but chiefly malicious, which set his pulse beating faster. 'The poor little thing was only too glad to come. He has been telling me all about it, and he *has* had a dull time with you. He said he had no idea that Wiswell could be so disagreeable.'

'Your trick was ingenious, I must confess. I am sorry to say I don't see much meaning in it,' said Lawford, with great dignity, since she seemed to expect him to say something.

'Of course you don't,' said Peril. 'My meaning was that I had something to say to you, and I could think of no other way of getting hold of you.'

'I should have been happy to call and see you, without any such elaborately concocted plot. A simple note would have sufficed to bring me.'

'I doubt it. But now that you are here——' she had proceeded steadily enough so far, now she began to falter and fidget with her watch-chain.

'Perhaps you will be kind enough to get your errand over. You are prodigal in gifts, I know. Perhaps you wish to present me with the Grange, now that you have bought it.'

'You must say whatever you like,' said Peril, casting her eyes down. 'I can have nothing to say in answer. I have heard that you have sold the Grange because you think of going abroad.'

'You have heard what is quite true.'

'And taking Humphrey with you?'

'Certainly.'

'And never coming back to England?'

'Never, if I can possibly help it.'

'And that you are going directly?'

'I hope to set off to-morrow.'

He saw that she breathed more quickly—that her eyes wavered and flickered: she looked round the room—towards the door—at him—everywhere; and at last, almost in a whisper, said:

'Will you take me with you?'

He looked at her for a few moments, and then, resolutely crushing down the wish to clasp her in his arms and cover her face with

61—2

kisses, said, in as flippant a tone as he could call to his aid:

'Another practical joke, I suppose. You have taught me that it is best to have no dealings at all with you; but if I were obliged to do so, I should ask for a sign or token that you meant what you said.'

'Any sign, any token that you please to name!' she exclaimed, holding out her hands appealingly. 'Lay down your condition, and let it be what it may, I accept it.'

'You said something of the kind before, I remember; and when it came to the test, you—slapped me in the face.'

'If you do not utterly refuse, give me a condition,' she said, very pale, and, as he saw, trembling from head to foot.

'The poor old Grange is in a somewhat dilapidated condition just now,' he observed. 'I'm only thinking of an instance, you know, since you won't let me go home without one.

It is hardly in a state to receive a fastidious lady ; though a man's wife, who cared more for him than his house, might find it habitable. Suppose, for example, that to-morrow you bring Humphrey home—and remain there yourself.'

Peril abruptly turned away. Covering her face with her hands, but not before he had seen the flood of red that rushed over her pale face, she put her elbows on the mantelpiece, and buried her face in her arms, in silence.

'Aha !' said he, after a prolonged pause. 'I thought, when it came to realities, there would be a difficulty. Good-evening.'

'Paul — stop !' she said suddenly, and turned to him with her face whiter than ever. 'I said, anything. I will bring Humphrey to-morrow, and—if you will let me—I will stay.'

'You must not think me a perfect bear if

I say, we will let the bargain stand so, and that, *when* you come, you will be welcome—provided you do not come to buy off your part of the contract with a thousand pounds or so.'

' Paul !'

'Why not ? What you have done once, you may do again.'

' You do not believe me. I cannot be surprised, but I am afraid of you when you look at me like that. Have you forgotten that you once gave me this ?'

She put her hand to her throat, and unclasped the little gold chain he had given her.

'Since you do not believe me—and I think, from your looks, you do not want to believe me,' she said—' I would like you to take it back, please.' And she held it out to him.

Paul, half involuntarily, held out his hand,

took the end of the chain, and she held
the other; and thus, for a few moments,
they stood, before all was over for bliss or
bale; before any irrevocable words had been
spoken. Paul felt as if life were coursing fast
away. The clock ticked—surely never was
so strange an interview!—the rain dripped
from the eaves outside, and fell with a splash
upon the walk. Suppose to-morrow never
came for some of them. Deathlike stillness
prevailed, save for these two sounds. Why
had she been at the trouble of doing all this,
unless it was, as she said, to make amends?
Bah! because everything that she wanted
was indispensable one moment, almost loath-
some the next. The inevitable moment,
which must bring parting for ever and ever,
or reconciliation, was hurrying, striding towards them. Each tick of the clock heralded
its approach. From afar it came; from the
depths and the abysses of their mutual des-

tinies. And neither he nor she could give a guess as to whether it would bring them happiness or misery.

If he might only clasp her in his arms, as she stood there, drooping, and say that all should be forgiven—if she would only love him a little! And be served as she had served him before! Peril that she was, who could do nothing that was not dangerous. Had she not driven him nearly mad with anxiety this very day, and all to get an interview which she might have had by writing a note, and saying she wanted to speak to him? Drip, drip, from the eaves—tick, tick, went the clock; and they stood, holding each one end of a little gold chain, looking like fools, doubtless.

'Am I to take it, and wish you goodnight?' he said at last; and looking at her, he met her eyes, and saw that she was all a-tremble, and fluttering with agitation.

Her voice came quiveringly, and still she kept her hold of the chain :

'Let me understand you clearly. When I bring Humphrey to-morrow, I shall have told my uncle that I am not coming back. Will you refuse to let me stay ?'

'*When* you bring Humphrey, and express a desire to share our shelter, it will receive you, and give you what welcome it can,' he rejoined, still sceptically.

'Forgive me if I seem to importune you. Do I understand that you will let me try to make amends, as it is my only wish to do, for—oh, Paul, Paul, Paul !'

She sobbed out his name with a mixture of anguish and love and joy, as she sprang to the arms which he opened to her, and flung her own about his neck.

'You will let me come—you will let me come !'

'Let you come—ah, Peril, only put your

foot within my door, and it shall fly open to
receive you.   Only enter, and we will see—
we will see who shall make amends.'   .

*   *   *   *   *

Natures—of human beings—do not change,
though they may modify.   It is not pretended that Margaret Hankinson, in her
married life, was never made to feel that she
had given up much more to her husband
than he ever understood, or ever gave up
for her.   It is not for a moment asserted that
Paul Lawford had tamed once for all the
woman who had at last come to his feet; but
he had awakened in her a love that was
stronger than her fierceness or her selfishness; and with that love for a lever, he would
probably find that he could compass most
things that he wished.   As mortal lots are
cast, those of these four persons were not set
in evil places, though the paths of the two
couples will, as time goes on, drift farther and

farther apart. Each will cling to his or her own. None will be quite able to forget the strife that once was amongst them, or that circumstances were merciful in taking their fates out of their own hands.

THE END.

BILLING AND SONS, PRINTERS, GUILDFORD.
G. C. & Co.

Lightning Source UK Ltd.
Milton Keynes UK
UKHW022024230123
415854UK00023B/269

9 781164 920502